# Find Happiness Now
# Be Do Have

## The Cure for the Great Unknown American Epidemic

### By
### Miami Phillips

*"Miami Phillips has written an important book that looks beneath the surface, giving the reader insights and practical advice. For anyone wanting to be, to do and to have, Miami does an excellent job explaining the hidden motivators in your life and how you can use that insight to your advantage."*
Richard Reardon President, R&R Business Development and Author of "The Business Development Guide" www.richardreardon.com.

*"Being, Doing, Having. Three common words that Miami Phillips takes to deeper meanings. This book takes only a few hours to read, and it provides a path to a happier, more peaceful existence. BeDoHave offers a plain-spoken guide to the happiness that lies within us all. Put it into faithful practice, and BeDoHave can change your life forever."*
Dr. John Stephenson Certified Professional Coach, Author of Intentional Change and mediocre chess player

© Copyright Miami Phillips
3rd Printing September 2006
2nd Printing October 2005
All Rights Reserved.

ISBN: 1-59453-968-5

VicToria Freudiger, Editor - Publisher
**Entry Way Publishing**
www.entrywaypublishing.com
entrywaypublish@aol.com

© Copyright 2004, Miami Phillips
Bookman Publishing
ISBN: 1-59453-384-9
All Rights Reserved.

No part of this book may be reproduced, stored in a retrieval system, or transmitted by any means, electronic, mechanical, photocopying, recording, or otherwise, without written permission from the author, Miami Phillips

**HAVE**

| | |
|---|---|
| Introduction To Have | 152 |
| Five Steps To A Great Life | 157 |
| How Do I Keep Moving? | 159 |
| What If? | 161 |
| Don't Look Back | 163 |
| Make Room | 165 |
| Resist Nothing | 167 |
| Create A Life Equation | 170 |
| Give A Little, Get A Lot | 174 |
| Are You Successful? | 176 |
| About Goals | 181 |
| More About Goals | 183 |
|     Reality #1. There Is A Price | 189 |
|     Reality #2. Keep Going | 191 |
|     Reality #3. Natural Laws | 193 |
|     Reality #4. Define The Dream | 195 |
| Choices Make Your Life | 198 |
| The Beginning | 204 |
| | |
| Acknowledgments | 205 |
| | |
| Final Thoughts | 207 |
| | |
| About The Author | 208 |

*Linda,*
*Thanks DeDe Hoover can change your life! Let it - Love Mom*

**To my lovely wife, Michele Marie, and our two sons, Ian and Ryan.**

*Where would I be without you?*

## **Introduction To Be Do Have**

You hold in your hands the cure for an unknown American epidemic. It might even be a world epidemic, but I live in the USA and know the epidemic best.

It is not our fault, but we can overcome the dilemma. We do not need to raise millions of dollars to research and combat it. We don't have to all come together and hold a candlelight vigil, although I am sure that would be very nice.

To cure this epidemic takes only two people: You and me. If we can cure ourselves, we can show others how to do the same. Soon, a neighborhood will be cured; then a city, a state, and then, all of America. At this point, we can help the world.

The epidemic is unhappiness. It has gradually snuck up on us and we didn't even see it coming. Unhappiness is so pervasive that now we forget what it was like to be filled with joy. At one time, we knew. We are born knowing joy and happiness. Think of a baby. A baby is the definition of joy. What happened to our joy and happiness? Where has it gone? Who have we allowed to steal our happiness from us?

We were conditioned before we were born and the result is a way of life called Do-Have-Be. Let's look at it.

How do we get to a career? The answer is: We go to school, learn a trade, and then we go out to the marketplace and get a job in that field.

Perhaps, we join the family business and learn what our family has always done. Maybe a job was available when we needed one. On the other hand, there are those who were at the right place, during the right time, and now it provides them an income.

Usually, as we work our way into more income, we become complacent. How many people love what they are doing? How many people have a job regularly just for the money but convinces themselves otherwise? The money we earn is used to buy stuff. We buy cars, clothes, houses, memberships, schools, and even friends like there is no tomorrow.

All of our lives are conditioned by advertising and through our television programs. We are also conditioned through our parents and the methods they use in order to raise us. Our peers have hurt us. We have been taught to believe if we Do something, we can Have stuff. When we Have enough stuff, then we can Be somebody.

I remember a saying that I heard while I was a bartender in the restaurant business. People would come into the bar and say, "Let's get drunk and Be somebody!" What is wrong with who we are?

We are all working very hard to Be somebody. Are you? Also, we believe that happiness comes when we get to Be that person that has all that stuff.

Here is the problem. There is always more stuff to have. In other words, we can never actually Be somebody because there is always more to Do when we get to where we think we had to go.

Very few people are happy. Who do you know that actually has enough time and is satisfied with the money they have?

No matter how much money people have, there is always more to acquire.

This has created a whole new set of problems. One of the biggest problems we have created is the idea of scarcity... as in there is not enough (money, jobs, things) to go around. So now, we must compete for more.

In my opinion, this is an epidemic and we have to cure it before we spin out of control.

In my heart, I believe that there is a cure. All the great teachers throughout history have told us of this cure. It is simple. Turn the formula around to Be-Do-Have instead of Do-Have-Be.

This book is how to Be-Do-Have.

The book is in three sections: Be, Do and Have.

Read it any way you like. Start at the beginning. Pick a topic that attracts you from the contents. Start from where you open the book. It matters not. What matters is that you do it.

Cure yourself. Afterwards, give someone else the cure.

## **Why This? Why Now? Why Me?**

This book is in response to a need that I had in 1997. At that time in my life, in the beginnings of a spiritual discovery, I knew not where to begin. In the library there was no "Spirituality for Dummies."

What was needed was a step-by-step tutorial explaining how to start down the path leading to the life, which I was desperately seeking. This type of life was to be the answer to the questions that were building within me.

Questions such as:

> Why am I here?
> How do I know who I really am?
> What is it I am supposed to be doing?
> Why am I not happy?
> Why can't I get what I want no matter how hard I work?

I am not claiming to have all of these answers contained here. This book would be much more expensive if that were the case! However, since these questions have been asked for as long as man has memory, there have been many, many people who have passed down their opinions and ideas to us.

This work is my compilation of many of these teachers; mixed in with an interpretation of those I found which work for me and for many of my coaching clients over the last five years.

A large part of the BeDoHave formula is faith. The word faith has many different meanings. My purpose in this work is not to convince you, change your mind or tell you what to think. This is not a religious book. However, since I talk about Higher Power, Universal Power, and God, it might be important to let you know how I live my faith.

I believe passionately that we are a part of the energy of life. In addition, I believe that everything we do affects everything else because we are part of it. By the same definition, we are affected by everything else, and we hold some responsibility for it.

When I write of Higher Power, or Universal Power, I am referring to 'everything that is' power to which we all have access.

Take your time to get the most from this work. There are many topics, with numerous worksheets, which will help you answer your own questions. I would suggest this work be done slowly, with great thought and care taken on each, and every, task.

Some of the exercises in this book will not be easy to finish. In fact, they might take years to polish. Some will evolve all of your life.

# ❦ Be ❧

Until you make peace with who you are, you'll never be content with what you have.

Doris Mortman

## **Be Who You Are**

This is the story of a journey, my journey. By sharing what I have gone through, my hope is that you might be able to find shortcuts for your own path and growth towards what you have defined as success for you.

In 1996, I was financially bankrupt, emotionally depressed, and was desperately searching for answers.

As I write this book, five years later, I am able to report that my wife and I own a beautiful horse farm. A lovely lake surrounds our property. We have financial and emotional reserves. Life is perfect!

Here is the story of how that came to pass. In this book, I will share some of the lessons that we learned along the way.

As you read, keep a writing utensil, a highlighter or two, and a journal or notebook. Make notes, do the exercises, and highlight what strikes you. Personal growth is not an immediate process, but a slow steady achievement, accomplished one step at a time.

There is a lot of information directly related to changing your life. Keep the parts that speak to you. Other parts might not make sense now, but they will later. You can return again and again until the lessons are learned, and your life is perfect too!

Please note: I take the word Self very seriously. Wherever you read this word in my book, it will be

# CONTENTS

Introduction to Be Do Have ... ix
Why This? Why Now? Why Me? ... xii

## BE

Introduction To Be ... 1
Be Who You Are ... 2
Simplify ... 7
Five Steps To The Good Life ... 9
Your Choice, Your Life ... 12
Possible Solutions To Challenges ... 14
Start With Values ... 17
The Power Of Benchmarks ... 19
Needs Are A Challenge ... 33
Integrity (Or A Cup Full Of Holes) ... 38
Living With Integrity ... 40
Draw The Line ... 43
Searching For Happiness? Look Within ... 46
How Fast Is Your Rate Of Change? ... 48
We Are What We Think ... 50
Today Could Be Your Last – Act Like It ... 53
The Present Is A Gift ... 55
Gremlins ... 59
Where Is Your Place? ... 62
Change Is Good ... 63
Attraction – A Way Of Life ... 66
How Good Do We Have To Be? ... 69
Be Who You Are – Final Thoughts ... 71

-v-

## DO

| | |
|---|---|
| Introduction To Do | 72 |
| Do What You Love | 73 |
| Jump Out Of Bed | 75 |
| Cricket In The Wall | 79 |
| Sometimes Changes Are Forced | 83 |
| Finding What We Love To Do | 88 |
| Five Magic Words | 93 |
| Habits | 96 |
| Comfort Zone | 101 |
| Change | 103 |
| Major And Minor | 106 |
| Brain Dump Activity | 111 |
| Time | 113 |
| Change Your Reality | 116 |
| Coping vs. Creating | 118 |
| As Soon As | 121 |
| Procrastination | 123 |
| Die In This Ditch? | 126 |
| Take Action | 128 |
| Action Requires Consistency | 131 |
| Dream, Act And Maintain | 133 |
| Adapt As You Need And Plow Ahead | 134 |
| Maintain It! | 136 |
| Now, Let Go | 138 |
| Want Money? You Got It! | 141 |
| Limited Beliefs | 143 |
| Dream Big | 146 |
| Final Words For Doing | 148 |

capitalized and stand alone, as in *your Self*. Much of the personal growth path requires the ability to understand, encourage and validate your Self. If we all took care of our Selves, the world would be an amazing place. Even more amazing than it already is!

---

*T*  *he most important step to creating a perfect life is to Be who you are.*

---

Not too long ago, (and maybe even today in some areas) to talk about Being and Presence would have caused some nervous laughter. No longer is it uncommon, as more and more people are asking the question: Who Am I? and Why am I here?

Let's look for ways to answer those two questions.

Merriam Webster dictionary defines Being as:
Main Entry: [1]**be·ing** Function: *noun* **1 a**: the quality or state of having existence **b** (1): something conceivable as existing (2): something that actually exists (3): the totality of existing things **c**: conscious existence.

For the purpose of our discussion, we choose **c**: conscious existence. *Being is conscious existence.*

Being is not static. Being is dynamic, ever-changing, ever-evolving. In reality, you never just "are," you simply be.

---

*B*e *what is right for you in that moment. Be real in your beliefs, in your thoughts, and in your actions.*

---

There are three major steps to be taken on the road to fulfilling our definition of Being as conscious existence.

1. **Choose Your Life**:
Being is about choosing as much as anything else. We all have choices to make each and every second. These choices create our lives, and create who we are. For example: if I choose to be happy as much as possible - would that change my life? You bet.

2. **Define Yourself**:
In a world full of strong outside influences, each of us must have an internal means of making decisions to keep our Selves strong and whole. By defining and clarifying benchmarks such as values, integrity, and how we know we are successful, we can hold up any decision that we need to make against them for truth and answers when required. There is much more to come on this subject.

3. **Live the Truth**:
We all have to live with what is truth to us. We all improve our lives by being true to ourselves as we have defined it. This does not mean the definitions cannot change, as they must while we grow. If truth to you means always being in integrity, then every time you tell a lie, you tear at the very fabric that makes up your life.

## *L*ife is perfect.

The very first thing most people think of is: "I am not perfect." No, you are not. Neither am I perfect. However, life itself is perfect and we will discover that soon.

This is the truth. The one thing that is absolutely without question is: The way your life is today depends completely upon one thing and one thing only: You.

This will entail You and your thoughts, as well as You and your actions, and You and your choices.

After you understand everything that happens - happens because you asked for it in some way, there is a lesson to be learned, or an opportunity to see. As soon as you understand this, you will begin to create your own life. *It is not so much what happens to you, as your response or reaction that makes up your world.*

This book is meant to be a collection of ideas and thoughts, which allow you to understand ways and means to create your own life to the extent you are willing to work at it. Creating life is not an easy task and it was never meant to be easy. In fact, life is quite difficult.

The challenges and problems we all face on a daily basis allow us to grow emotionally, spiritually, and mentally.

Without challenges, we would all stagnate and wither away. Some people, who ignore their challenges, actually do wither away, so to speak.

What makes the difference in someone who creates their life and someone who does not? The difference is in the manner each individual chooses to face up to the difficulties of life. The pain that we all face meeting and overcoming these obstacles is how we learn, and grow. Understand this concept and as a result, you will see each and every challenge as another opportunity to create your life exactly as you would like.

---

*Create your life. You have that power.*

---

My mission is to have every person realize the power of conscious choice.

Here are a few exercises and stories that I pray will help you somewhere along the line.

## **Simplify**

In the years between 1990 and 1997, we lived on a 36-foot sailboat. First, we spent almost two years building the boat; and then we sailed over 12,000 miles up and down the East Coast from New York to St. Martin in the Caribbean.

We lived simply. Washing was done in old cisterns or buckets or whatever we could find to do our clothes. We got our water from wherever we could; sometimes filling up containers from old wells with a rope and five gallon buckets. Then we would ferry the water in our little dingy out to the boat at anchor and fill up our tanks. Our 100-gallon water supply could easily last two weeks or more.

Our meals consisted of seafood caught by spear. We ate a lot of local produce, (such as cabbage as it kept for a long time without refrigeration.) Electricity came from batteries that we charged by using our small diesel engine.

---

*Life was good. Our world was contained in 36 feet.*

---

No phone, no mail, no bills, no TV and no car (except when we would stay somewhere for more than a couple of months – then, we would buy a clunker.)

Of course, as always there were tradeoffs. Sometimes it was a LONG way to the store. We depended upon ourselves, as help was not always near. Soon, we learned that we had better get along with the others on the boat.

My wife, Shelly and I talk about those years, and sometimes long for that simplicity. Life was full. The good times were awesome and the bad times were awful but we knew the good would return.

Our goal is to return to that simplicity as much as possible. We do our best to keep it now amid the hectic pace our lives seem to have. My family and I chose to live in this way for a set period of time to ensure the income that we require to live without struggling.

Our goal is in sight.

---

*All of us should do our best to simplify as much as possible.*

---

Here are a few tips on how to simplify your life:
- Live each moment to the fullest. Enjoy it.
- Learn why it is called the present.
- Do your best and trust that all will be well.
- Help is available from places you cannot see.
- Find your core values. Write them down and use them as a guide to make conscious choices every minute of every day.

Doing these exercises will create a future that serves your soul and helps you be your Self.

## **Five Steps To The Good Life**

There are many ways and means to accomplish whatever you want done. However, I have found that the most successful ways are so subtle and simple that they are usually overlooked.

As I try to decide what projects to work on here at our horse farm, it is so very easy to become overwhelmed with the big picture. How can I build a barn that big? Where will all the money come from to pay for it? How do I clear 20 acres of land and turn it into pasture? And so on, and so on.

Yesterday, as I was feeling a bit overwhelmed, I took a rake and went out to the pasture and spread piles of horse manure. Several wonderful things happened. First, I got the manure spread, which helped to fertilize the field, lower the fly and insect population, and made for fewer piles for us to step in. Secondly, I realized that this might be a great job for our four-year-old who will love knocking down those piles.

The most important benefit was that I was able to very much enjoy just being in the pasture and making a contribution toward our ultimate goals. My mind was free to smell the unique odors of horse ranching and the outside air. It was wonderful listening to the horses communicating. I enjoyed hearing the birds and the geese down by the lake, and watching the dog searching for whatever it is that dogs hunt.

*In other words, I was able to take the time to be grateful for what is here and now. I completely stopped thinking about the future, which caused me to be less overwhelmed. And this caused me to be able to get something done.*

We all want everything right now. This can cause two problems:
1. You can become overwhelmed with the immensity of the required tasks.
2. When you get what you want, a hunger still remains. There is always something else to want. If a person is not careful, they will go through life always hungry, but stuffed so full you are bloated. Metaphorically speaking that is--

Try this formula for living the good life:

1. **Above all else: Be yourself:**
   Do not try to be anyone else. Be uniquely you and take great pleasure in that.

2. **Do what you love to do:**
   If your life is made up of struggle, look at that struggle and ask yourself: what is the cause of the struggle? Are you doing things you do not want to do?

3. **Gratitude opens the door for all else:**
   Be continually grateful for all that you have. The things that you already have are gifts. If you and I were to talk today, how many things could you name for which you are thankful?

4. **Set your goals and intent. Afterwards, take the steps necessary to achieve them:**
   Communicate your dreams to the Universal Power and follow through on your part.

5. **Let go of the outcome:**
   What control do you have anyway? If you are enjoying being who you are, and you are enjoying doing what you love, anything that comes afterwards is a complete blessing. Why worry about it? Just make it happen.

These five steps are the basis of all the personal coaching that I do. I have seen people 'get' this and then by practicing the concepts, their lives really changed. Go ahead and create yours.

## **Your Choice**
## **Your Life**

Sometimes, life can throw a lot at you. What is the answer to dealing with unexpected surprises or events in your life? The answer is to choose well.

Are things not going your way? Do people seem to get on your nerves? Maybe the kids, or the boss is being a pain in the neck, or the car does not want to start.

---

*In these situations, one thing makes all the difference in the outcome.*

---

You. How you look at and perceive each happenstance in your life makes up your life.

Ask your Self this question: Can you believe every single event in your life happens for a reason? Can you believe that the reason is good, not otherwise?

If you answered, "*yes*" to either or both of these questions, and you look to each and everything, which occurs in your life to find the good in it, then you will find gold.

If you answered "no," sometimes, you will find gold, and sometimes, you will find fear, anger, hate, or jealousy.

*Be Do Have*

This is how we control our lives. It is as simple as deciding whether we look for good or bad in each and every event in every day.

From the time of our birth to our deaths, we create our lives by making choices; from getting out of bed grumpy or smiling, to having orange juice or water for breakfast. You can choose to listen to something motivational as you drive in your car or you can listen to a news program.

And you can always be fascinated by every single thing – or you can be frustrated.

---

*Your choice. Your life.*

---

*Be Do Have*

## **Possible Solutions To Challenges**

Are you having trouble believing that you have been given all the power needed to create whatever you want in your life? Do you consciously create your own life?

Here are four possible reasons you might be challenged:

1. You are unable to define what you actually want:

One of the reasons it is so critically important to define exactly what you want is the ability to communicate your wants to the Universe. You can create what you want but not by yourself. We are all one, and there is a Universal Power that must be called on to help. If you have a problem with the term Universal Power, how about God, or Gaia, or anything else that suits you? We are all energy and everything in the world is made of energy. Surely there must be a source of all energy, and we are all a part of that source. I know that we can tap into this energy. I do it daily.

This does not have to be about the idea of a Higher Power. Or it can if that suits you.

---

*What you believe is totally up to you.*

---

If you know exactly what you want and you take steps towards a goal with good intentions, help is waiting for you.

Events will happen that you might call coincidence, chance or luck - there is no such thing.

Now try this thought: Everything happening to you is created by you. Fun thought, is it not? (Of course it is only fun if you are enjoying your life!)

2.  Your wants are not in line with your values:

Your values are the ideals by which you live. You might even die for these values if need be. Have you defined those values?

If your values are family and relationships and you are telling the Universe you want money at the cost of those relationships, it is highly unlikely you will achieve either. However, if your value is relationships, and you work on relationships until you have all you want in that area, then you can begin to work on the money part.

3.  You are not taking action steps toward your goal:

*You can want all you like, but the Universe will not lift a finger unless you do.*

Likewise, if you stop, the Universe stops too. This is why you cannot quit no matter what happens, unless you change your goals. There is nothing wrong with changing goals. This is why you are given free choice.

4. You are not *being who you are*:

I see an epidemic in the world today that no one has really discussed much. A majority of the people is walking around *doing* something so they can *have* stuff, so they can *be* somebody. For instance, you might be working (*doing*) a job you do not like, so you can *have* money, so you can *have* a nice house, car, and other stuff. As soon as you have the stuff, you can *be* an important somebody defined as someone who has all that stuff.

In reality, if you gave up all the stuff (gulp!) just *be* who you are comfortable being, and work (*do*) at what brings you joy, something amazing will happen; you will get (*have*) everything that you need.

Does that mean you would be rich? It might be you do not need to be rich. Of course rich is defined in more ways than financial.

---

*D*efine who you are with values and vision.

---

## **Start With Values**

Goals have somehow slipped in my priorities. Vision, on the other hand, is gaining in importance. The difference between goals and vision is a little challenging to explain, but it has to do with too much rigidity in one's life, dealing too much in "shoulds" instead of "wants" and loss of vision due to short-term desires.

Vision is what your world will look like when you have achieved your life's goals. A powerful vision will always pull you forward. The prospect of seeing that vision become a reality will spring you out of bed in the morning. A vision is what calls you to be your best. A great vision can seem impossible, or at least unreachable, but at the same time, it can seem to be clear as a bell to you.

Goals, on the other hand, might be what you have when you don't have a vision. Goals are great for keeping you moving in a certain direction, a way to get something done. They are often set as a way to have a better future. If your life is not the way you want it today, you are likely to set goals to make it better tomorrow. The problem with this is you are living for tomorrow and not living for today.

---

*So – how do you find your vision? You don't. It finds you.*

---

If you can see a way of serving or helping others in a manner very rewarding and fulfilling for you, then you have a vision. For example, my vision is a world that understands our incredible ability to live our lives completely happy simply by choice.

Whether you do or do not have your vision at this time, one of the most powerful ways to accelerate the reality of a vision is to attract it to you. Work on your Self. Make your life as perfect as you can. The power of personal growth cannot be underestimated. When you are confident of who you are, with needs taken care of, boundaries in place to protect you, and your values clearly defined to enable you to make the thousands of choices available to you each and every day – you become incredibly attractive. Life is all about attraction. People, things, visions are all attracted to these kinds of people.

---

*Values are the place to start.*

---

Know and define your values and complex decisions will become easy. Doubt will be eliminated. With your values defined, your Self will be defined. You will begin to know who you are.

## The Power Of Benchmarks
### Decision-Making Made Easy

As you proceed along your chosen path, each and every minute brings an opportunity to make a decision that could possibly affect the rest of your life.

For instance, you could decide not to breathe. That would affect the rest of your life. You could decide to take a risk and step out of your comfort zone to speak to the person of your dreams standing next to you in line at the grocery store. You might even find that this particular person could possibly be looking for you. Would that change your life?

How about a decision more consciously made? What if you thought that you needed to move to a new place, find new work, find a new mate, or thousands of other life altering decisions you could make?

How do you make those decisions? What tools do you use in order to help you make a decision that will affect the rest of your life, and those lives you feel responsible for such as your spouse and children?

---

*T**he first tool is Values. Your values are who you are. To know your values is to know your core definition.*

---

*Be Do Have*

Define your top four or five values. Answer the following questions to help you explore values that are most compelling to you.

Jump ahead to the end of your life. You are looking back on a long life and asking your Self these questions.

---

What are the three most important lessons in your life, which you have learned that you would pass on to others?

1. _____
_____
_____
_____
_____

2. _____
_____
_____
_____
_____

3. _____
_____
_____
_____
_____

Wait! Did you answer the question -- or did you skip the question? Here is a secret to the incredible power of personal growth. There is no secret!

---

*P*ersonal growth, personal development, and finding your path all take work.

---

You must do the work yourself. If you are just curious, then fine, go ahead and skip the exercises. If you are serious as I am about your Self, then stop now and answer this and every question. Do every exercise. Work at it! No one will do this for you. (But you already knew that didn't you?)

Next question is ...

Why are these lessons so important to you?

1. _____
   _____
   _____
   _____
   _____

2. _____
   _____
   _____
   _____
   _____

3. _____
   _____
   _____
   _____
   _____

*Be Do Have*

Name someone you deeply respect. _____
Describe three qualities you most admire in this person:

1. _____

_____

_____

_____

2. _____

_____

_____

_____

3. _____

_____

_____

_____

*Be Do Have*

Describe you when you were at your best. For example: volunteering to raise money for a kid's halfway house, being a Mom or a Dad, coaching kids' sports.

My best was when_____

_____

_____

_____

_____.

What is the one statement that people would say about you, which captures who you really were in your life? For example: He was always laughing and helping others laugh.

They said that I:_____

_____

_____

_____

_____.

Values provide a source of inspiration and meaning that cannot be taken away from us.

---

*Deeply held values fuel the energy on which purpose is built.*

---

Values make decision-making much easier and much less emotional.

*Be Do Have*

Utilizing the previous statements, choose 3-5 values that reflect the way you want to live. You can use any words you like. These are just examples for you.

| What gives me purpose? | | |
|---|---|---|
| Authenticity | Balance | Commitment |
| Compassion | Compassion | Concern for others |
| Courage | Creativity | Empathy |
| Excellence | Fairness | Faith |
| Family | Freedom | Friendship |
| Generosity | Genuineness | Happiness |
| Harmony | Health | Honesty |
| Humor | Integrity | Kindness |
| Knowledge | Loyalty | Openness |
| Perseverance | Respect for Others | Responsibility |
| Security | Serenity | Service to Others |
| | | |

This exercise can be frustrating. All of the words might seem like values. Choose the 4 or 5 <u>most</u> important to you.

1. _____
2. _____
3. _____
4. _____
5. _____

Congratulations! Now you have a benchmark for making unemotional decisions. If in doubt, run your decisions by your values. If your decision does not meet all your values, you must consider it very carefully. If you do something that does not honor your values, then you are tearing apart your Self, and doing something that goes against who you are. You can do it, but at what price?

---

*Defining values is not simple. It can take a long time to feel comfortable with your choices.*

---

There is a strong pull to select items that we call needs instead of values.

A value is something that calls to you. It feels naturally important to you. Many times you can go back to your childhood and clearly see your values by what you liked most as a child. For instance: peace, passion, creativity, friends, family and honesty are values. You will find yourself naturally drawn to your values.

A need is something you must have in order to be your best. An example of a need would be time, space, money, love, information, food, exercise, or tools. Usually, you feel satisfaction when you get one of your needs met.

It is important to know the difference and to know exactly what you need as well as your values. Why? If you know your needs, you can focus on them one at a time, until they are met and satisfied. Those who do not satisfy needs consciously will unconsciously do whatever it takes to meet those needs. For example: If you are a person who needs attention, you *will get attention.* The attention you get unconsciously might be in the form of bad behavior just so that you are noticed.

After you know your values, making decisions about anything becomes much simpler. If you have four core values and you have a decision to make, simply look at it from the perspective of your values and ask yourself: *Will this answer bring me closer or farther away from my values?*

For example you have decided one of your values is family. Your boss offers you a promotion. With the promotion comes the requirement to spend five days a week traveling around the country. As you compare your decision against your values, you understand clearly that you will see your family only on weekends and will miss any events happening during the week. You tell your boss, "No thanks," and explain why.

Now you have a quality-of-life benchmark, which you can use for answering everything.

Is it that easy? Of course not; but, if you can work through and realize your needs and your values, then your life will become much more focused, and manageable. You will find yourself floundering much less and you will feel more in control.

You might find that you are married to the wrong person, or in the wrong occupation or living in the wrong place. This realization will bring a fear of change, which alone could stop you from wanting to live. What would you do? Use your values and your definitions of success for you to decide consciously what is best for you.

---

*Realize that understanding who you are could change your life a great deal.*

---

You might realize that you have been living someone else's values. Or, you may have been living by someone else's definitions of success.

After Values, the second tool is Definitions of Success. How can you achieve success if you do not know what it is for you?

Complete this sentence three times:

*I know I am being successful when I...*

This is not an easy exercise; so do not give up too quickly. After you define success for your Self, you have the power to make every decision count for that success and not against it. It is important that you define success in terms that you can control. For instance, the following are not in your control and therefore, subject to failure.

I know that I am successful when I...am financially independent.

I know that I am successful when...my wife loves me.

I know that I am successful when…my children grow up to be successful.

Turn these statements around to read:

I know that I am successful when I…live within my means and am able to do my best in order to ensure financial independence. Or, even better – have financial reserves.

I know that I am successful when I…do my best to earn my wife's love.

I know that I am successful when I…provide my children with the best opportunity in order to ensure their success however they define it.

Take a moment now to define what success is for you. After you know your definition of success, and your personal values, you have specific benchmarks that allow no questions as to whether you are reaching for the star that suits you.

I know that I am being successful when I:

1. _____

2. _____

3. _____

You now have the tools required to ensure every decision made is building a life based on your values and your definition of success.

---

*Y*ou *will be successful by your definition instead of someone else's. You will live by your values and not the values untrue for you.*

---

Here are my personal definitions as of this writing. Note that definitions of success change. As you are dynamic and ever-changing, your definitions will also change.

I know I am successful when I am excited about getting out of bed every day.

I know I am successful when I am able to give love freely without expectation.

I know I am successful when I have six months living expenses in reserve.

Notice that none of these statements are dependent on someone or something else. This is very important.

Having success defined means we all have a way of determining when we are beginning to move away from what is important in our life. We are able to control success. We will continue to work toward financial independence or wonderful relationships with others as a goal – but our happiness and success is not dependent on it.

## **Needs Are A Challenge**

Each of us has needs. Our needs are fulfilled either consciously or subconsciously. It is crucial to ensure our needs are being met and satisfied in the right way.

After this is accomplished, we will work on getting those needs met and our lives will be much simpler.

Here is an example. Let us say a person has a need to be touched. This is not an unhealthy need. This simply means they do much better if they have someone close to them who is aware of this need and often hugs them, or reaches for their hand. Do you see how everything this person does will be affected by this need? What would happen if this person was not aware of this need, and it was not met? What might they do unconsciously to get this need met?

Much of the crime today could be eliminated if we all had our needs met.

What would happen if this person were able to understand his/her needs? What if they went to their life partner and made a request for help by stating their needs and explaining how the need could be filled. Would someone who loves them do this if asked? Absolutely! They would go out of their way to touch their partner. And would that help meet this person's need? Again – yes, it would.

When your needs are met, you cannot believe how much it allows you to live your life more freely, and fully. Since you are not unconsciously working on needs, you can consciously work on the values that make you complete.

*Be Do Have*

What do you need most? To be heard, or loved or touched? Do you need to be individualistic like I do? How about money, success, health?

What needs do you have that might be steering your life more than necessary? How would your life be different if those needs were met – completely and fully? How would it feel?

Choose five top needs you have from the following list.

*Be Do Have*

Make every effort to consciously get your needs fulfilled. Just being aware of your needs will make a huge impact on your life.

## NEEDS LIST

**BE ACCEPTED**
Approved
Be included
Respected
Permitted
Be popular
Sanctioned
Cool
Allowed
Tolerated
**TO ACCOMPLISH**
Achieve
Fulfill
Realize
Reach
Profit
Attain
Yield
Consummate
Victory
**BE ACKNOWLEDGED**
Be worthy
Be praised
Honored
Flattered
Complimented
Be prized
Appreciated
Valued
Thanked
**BE LOVED**
Liked
Cherished

Esteemed
Held fondly
Be desired
Be preferred
Be relished
Be adored
Be touched
**BE RIGHT**
Correct
Not mistaken
Honest
Morally right
Be deferred to
Be confirmed
Be advocated
Be encouraged
Understood
**BE CARED FOR**
Get attention
Be helped
Cared about
Be saved
Be attended to
Be treasured
Tenderness
Get gifts
Embraced
**CERTAINTY**
Clarity
Accuracy
Assurance
Obviousness
Guarantees
Promises

Commitments
Exactness
Precision
**BE COMFORTABLE**
Luxury
Opulence
Excess
Prosperity
Indulgence
Abundance
Not work
Taken care of
Served
**TO COMMUNICATE**
Be heard
Gossip
Tell stories
Make a point
Share
Talk
Be listened to
Comment
Informed
**TO CONTROL**
Dominate
Command
Restrain
Manage
Correct others
Be obeyed
Not ignored
Keep status quo
Restrict

*Be Do Have*

**BE NEEDED**
Improve others
Be a critical link
Be useful
Be craved
Please others
Affect others
Need to give
Be important
Be material
**DUTY**
Obligated
Do the right thing
Follow
Obey
Have a task
Satisfy others
Prove self
Be devoted
Have a cause
**BE FREE**
Unrestricted
Privileged
Immune
Independent
Autonomous
Sovereign
Not obligated
Self-reliant
Liberated
**HONESTY**
Forthrightness
Uprightness
No lying

Sincerity
Loyalty
Frankness
No withholds
No perpetrations
Tell all
**ORDER**
Perfection
Symmetry
Consistent
Sequential
Checklists
Unvarying
Right-ness
Literal-ness
Regulated
**PEACE**
Quietness
Calmness
Unity
Reconciliation
Stillness
Balance
Agreements
Respite
Steadiness
**POWER**
Authority
Capacity
Results
Omnipotence
Strength
Might
Stamina

Prerogative
Influence
**RECOGNITION**
Be noticed
Be remembered
Be known for
Regarded well
Get credit
Acclaim
Heeded
Seen
Celebrated
**SAFETY**
Security
Protected
Stable
Fully informed
Deliberate
Vigilant
Cautious
Alert
Guarded
**WORK**
Career
Performance
Vocation
Press, push
Make it happen
A task
Responsibility
Industriousness
Be busy

Thanks to Thomas Leonard and CoachU

*Be Do Have*

> My top five needs are:
>
> 1. _____
> 2. _____
> 3. _____
> 4. _____
> 5. _____

Another important part of being who you are is integrity.

## **Integrity (Or A Cup Full Of Holes)**

As energetic beings, we are made up of 90% energy and 10% flesh, blood and bone. Okay, so I am guessing at the numbers, but do you see what I mean?

This is why all the Great Teachers say that we have so much control over what happens in our lives. It is all about the choices that we make. The choices we make affect the energy in the world around us.

We receive and give energy all day long. What we do with our energy is so very important to how our lives play out for us.

Think of your energy flowing into you like a cup. Perfection is a cup overflowing with this energy. With a full cup, not only do you have plenty of energy to take care of your Self - your health, mental and physical, your attitude, your thoughts, and your outlook; but also you will have extra energy to give away to those who are in need.

On the other hand, if you have holes in your cup, you won't be able to keep enough energy in the cup for you.

If you are losing more energy than you receive, where do you get the extra energy you require? At first, you pull in this energy from your reserves. When your reserves are exhausted, you begin to use the energy stored in your healthy cell tissue. Is it any wonder there is so much illness in the world?

What causes holes? Any negative action on your part, such as dishonesty, greed, jealousy, anger and hate can all cause huge holes. Negatives allow energy to be wasted.

Try today to start plugging those holes one by one. You will actually feel your energy level increase little by little, and your attitude on life will improve as well.

As a small example of this, think of promises you have made.

## Living With Integrity
## How to Handle Broken Promises

Each and every day, we all make promises. We make these promises in many different ways, and in a variety of forms. A promise can be as simple as, "I'll call you back," or as committing as, "I promise to get that done."

Often, we make promises and commitments without thinking through the time, effort and resources necessary to complete them. When this happens, someone feels as though they got the short end of the deal. Sometimes that person is you. More often it means someone else has been let down.

We all make promises, which we are unable to keep for whatever reason - it just happens. Maybe, we have too much going on and we really wanted to do what we committed to but simply could not get it done. If I am unable to fulfill a commitment, it becomes wasted energy because one of my top four values is integrity. When I make a promise or commitment hard to keep, it's emotionally painful. Many times my inability to perform an obligation or commitment affects me more than the person that I made the promise to in the first place.

I have learned to recognize when I am unable to meet a deadline, or a commitment, or to fulfill a promise and to take an additional crucial step. This step is simple, yet powerful. It allows me to maintain my integrity, and removes any feelings of guilt or worry I used to carry due to perceived lack of integrity on my part.

This simple step is forgiveness. I ask forgiveness of my Self or of the person to whom I am unable to fulfill a commitment. We are not always able to do what we say we are going to do. For whatever reason, we cannot always send a payment as we promised, finish a committed report, or complete a project by the date that we said we would.

However, we can, and should notify the party to whom we have committed and ask forgiveness. We then set up a payment plan, redefine the report due date or reset the project due date.

It is suggested that you take this step as soon as you see yourself unable to meet your commitments. Taking this step can make your life so much better by removing most of the worry and guilt feelings that normally accompany this loss of integrity. As soon as you recognize this situation, act immediately. Immediate action not only helps you, but it also communicates to the other party that you recognize and honor their basic right to know what is happening. They will respect you more for the help.

There is a way to solve the problem so that it never happens again.

---

*R*ecognize what you can and cannot do.

---

Consistently under-promise and over-deliver on all your commitments.

Another tool for being who you are, and keeping your energy full is boundaries and tolerations.

## **Draw The Line**
### **Boundaries and Tolerations**

Boundaries are an imaginary line around you that protect you, your Self, and what is important in your life. Tolerations are just what they seem: they are little or big things that we put up with every day while ignoring them for the most part because they are too low on our priority scale to do something about.

To work on these two energy-giving tools requires baby steps – every day.

First – tolerations. Make a list of all the things that you put up with in your life. Silly, small, or large, we all have things we tolerate on a constant basis.

Some examples are:
- Closets you can't get into
- Dings in your car
- A person who bothers you
- Scratches in your dining table
- Not making enough money
- Living where you don't want to live

As you make your list, think of all the energy that you spend, which has accumulated over time while you were thinking and dealing with this stuff. Actually, just getting these lists into the open will help you resolve some of them. Realize you cannot eliminate all of your tolerations, but you can certainly work on most.

As you make your list, decide which item on your list is the biggest energy drainer and attack that one first. The energy boost you will receive from solving one toleration will give you incentive to work on the next and the next. Pick one a day, or one a week and just get it accomplished.

Boundaries can impact your life more powerfully than tolerations. Boundaries are imaginary lines you place around yourself to protect you.

For instance, I have a boundary of no violence in my life. I first set a boundary of 'you can't hit me or abuse me in any way.' Afterward, I moved it out further to say, 'you can't yell or raise your voice, and I will not stay in an area where this is happening.' It was about this time that we removed all programmed TV from our lives. And finally, the boundary became: 'you can't get angry at me at all, because I would not do anything intentionally to make you angry. Therefore, I request you come to me and tell me what is going on so we can address it.' I have very, very little violence in my life, and this concept now extends to our children.

After you set this imaginary line around you, and stick to it, you will be amazed at how much better you feel, and how people will respect you for it. Some examples of boundaries are:
- No raising your voice to me.
- No accepting gossip from others.
- Not allowing others to denigrate or make fun of others in front of you.
- Not allowing rude or offensive language near you.

*Be Do Have*

ଔ Not allowing people or things to waste your time and energy.

Make a list of your own boundaries.

---

*S et boundaries, and eliminate tolerations and you will discover a surprising personal growth level. You will find more energy, more freedom of movement, less fear and more faith in yourself.*

---

You are you, and you need to take care of you.

| Begin now. Make your boundaries list here: |
|---|
| 1. _____ |
| 2. _____ |
| 3. _____ |
| 4. _____ |
| 5. _____ |

## **Searching For Happiness? – Look Within**

Happiness can be defined in as many ways as there are people doing the defining. I cringe when a client or an associate says, "I'll be happy when…"

Examine the following phrases:

I'll be happy when I get that promotion.
I'll be happy when I meet the person of my dreams.
I'd be happy if I had one million dollars.

These, and all the other "if I had" scenarios are following the same reasoning: that happiness is based on external circumstances.

If you base your happiness on external circumstances, you will continuously fail. There will always, always be another external circumstance. More than likely, there will always be another dollar, another job or another house. Some people will end up looking for (often unnecessarily) another partner. Or, there will be always something to come along that will seem better. An average thinker spends time thinking that there is always something else that they need.

To break this vicious cycle, we must find our happiness somewhere else. That somewhere else is within each one of us.

---

*We have been given everything we need to be happy. Happiness is a choice we make.*

---

So don't worry – Be Happy. Choose it.

Did you know your ability to choose might be dependant on outside forces?

## **How Fast Is Your Rate Of Change?**

Carolyn Myss wrote a great book, <u>Energy Anatomy</u>. In this book she states, "We are energetic beings with a material body."

Carolyn teaches that we are predominantly energy, and we have the ability to use this energy to maintain our physical, mental and emotional health.

One of the subjects that she discusses in depth is the *Tribe* and our relationship to one. She defines the Tribe as the group (or groups) into which you are heavily invested. In the beginnings of your life this is your family. Later, this tribe could be your circle of friends, church, or any other group that you give your energy to as a member.

Here is a great point to remember. When you invest in a tribe, you are a part of the tribe, and as such, you can only change at the speed of the tribe.

---

*This is so important that I want to repeat it. You can only change your Self at the speed of the tribe.*

---

This means you invest your beliefs in the same beliefs as the tribe. For instance, if the tribe believes that you must be married and have children by age 40, so will you. If the tribe believes that only a very few people ever earn a lot of money, and it is very difficult to do, then you are likely to believe the same ideas.

*Be Do Have*

However, when you are free of the tribe, and not tied into their beliefs, you are free to change at any rate you want. If you believe that you can heal immediately, and you are not tied to another belief such as healing takes doctors and medicine, then quite possibly, you can heal immediately.

The trade off includes feelings of belonging, safety in numbers, support, ability to shrug off responsibility, and all the other benefits of tribal membership, versus the fear of going at it alone and accepting all responsibility for your own decisions.

I choose to go my own way. I have chosen to accept responsibility for my actions (or my inactions.) In my case, when someone says to me – "You can't do that" – I just have to smile and say to myself, "I'm glad I am not part of that tribe!"

What tribe or tribes are you heavily invested in? Is it serving you well?

## **We Are What We Think**

We are what we think. Consider the following ideas…

Think and grow rich.

Where your thinking is, there is your experience.

That which I feared has come unto me.

Ask and ye shall receive.

One of the vital keys to the universe, to happiness, to peace and joy, is this thought process. You and I are able to construct our individual world by simply having faith, belief and control over our thought process. It is simple and difficult at the same time.

Are you having difficulty in your business? If you think you are, guess what…deep inside you are likely asking for difficulty in some way. If you don't like it, dig down until you find what it is and change it. How about your relationships with your family or friends, or your co-workers, or with your work, or your health?

---

*You and I have the power to direct our lives in any direction we wish to go.*

---

Some people believe that we are here on this planet in order to learn a lesson in our continued spiritual growth. We are not here for someone else to use, or to please someone else. They have that responsibility. Our role here on earth is to be who our soul cries out to be.

If you are true to your Self, everything else fits—like a glove. If you are not true to your Self or to your own soul, then nothing seems to fit. Everything might just be a little off somehow, a little out of balance, or out of sorts.

How will we know if we are in balance or not? Stop long enough to listen. Some call it meditation. Other people call it quiet time. Find a quiet place. Learn to clear your mind and let come what will. Make it a daily practice. It is hard to find 10 minutes to sit quietly, but your life will change if you do this exercise.

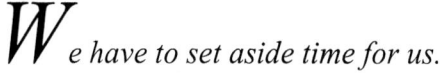

*We have to set aside time for us.*

Start today, and practice a little at a time.

Here are other ways to begin this process in order to enhance and/or to create your new world:

1. **Monitor your thoughts:**
   Look for any thinking that you may be doing, which is contrary to the way you want things to be. Eliminate those thoughts. Replace the contrary thoughts with a balanced thought in order to reinforce your new positive plan. A simple

example is to not think of what is going wrong, but change your thoughts to what is going right. Is the glass half full or half empty? There is a BIG difference!

2. **Take it easy on your Self:**
   Remove those things from your life that fill your head with ideas and thinking, which is counter-productive to your goals and positive thoughts. These might include TV, talk radio, newspapers, negative people and reading either negative or too much material. Replace these with positives like tapes and books on uplifting and motivating subjects of your choosing. Replace your negative friends.

3. **Keep a journal and record everything:**
   Clearly spell out how things will be. You are giving your subconscious mind directions on how to work while you sleep.

4. **Monitor your conversations:**
   Be careful of what you say. When you speak, you are telling the Universe what to do. Speak well of your Self and of others. Be positive, supporting and helpful - or don't speak at all.

How soon do you want to get started?

## **Today Could Be Your Last Act like It**

There is one thing, which is absolutely for certain in this life: you are not going to make it out alive. If we say we will live 75 years as an average (a guess on my part,) then you can count how many springs you have left. Based on these numbers, how many springs do you have left?

We get so caught up in working and worrying about tomorrow, we forget to enjoy today.

---

*Enjoy today as if there will be no tomorrow.*

---

All that we can do about tomorrow is to set some intentions of where we might like to be. Consciously make every choice that you can based on your values. Leave the results up to the Universe. We believe that we can control the future, but this is a joke. If you really consider how little control you have, you would spend much less time worrying and spend more time staying here, in the present moment.

---

*Every minute given to us is a gift to be treasured and savored.*

---

Don't risk being in the position one day of looking back on your life and wishing you could live certain moments over again. Don't end up wishing you had done more, been bolder, spent more time with loved ones, traveled, adventured, and really lived.

No matter where you are in your life, accept the present as the gift that it is. Make the most of your life…right now.

## **The Present Is A Gift**

To have our cake and eat it too. Is this truly what we all would like? We utilize our energy to attract exactly the life we desire. We use visualization techniques, set some goals, live for our vision, and make plans. Some of us keep journals in order to see how well we are doing. Other people even talk to his or her inner Self.

Time passes. One day, we realize that we are living the exact life or even better than we had dreamed. If we do not have everything that we asked for, we may realize that we actually may have more than we imagined.

Our environment nurtures us and our relationships are supportive and loving. The workplace is not actually work but an expression of our soul.

And - we have absolutely not enough time in the day to do it all! One day, we will wake up and say: "Wow! This is great, but maybe, I should go back to when I had nothing. At least then, I had some time to enjoy my life."

I have to admit I feel that way sometimes. How do we deal with this? What can we do to manage all the events, the meetings, the to-do's, the kids, the business, the meals, the house, the friends and all the other stuff that comes with a full life?

The answer is - by being in the present. If we could but learn to live completely in the present moment, life would be easier to manage. There would be no problems, only challenges popping up to be dealt with immediately from the heart in the best way possible. There would be no worry about tomorrow. How can you worry about tomorrow when you are fully engaged in this moment? The past carries no weight as it is gone and the past matters not one bit in the present.

Sounds easy doesn't it? Simply keep your thoughts in the present moment and life will become a piece of cake.

Why is it so difficult to stay present, and out of the future or the past? Not too many years back, my mind would have laughed at the following reasoning.

The challenge to living in the present comes from our old friend, ego. Our ego lives in constant fear of being ignored or even worse – being put away forever. The ego desires to be heard and speaks the loudest in our minds. Mankind's ego knows that if it allowed the mind to be quiet long enough, we (as our **Self**) would know the joy and peace that comes from just **being**. An ego must keep the mind so busy that we cannot hear our soul because of all the noise.

Our minds are simply a tool to be used. Egos control of our minds for most of us. Instructions to the mind are simple. Do whatever you must, but do not be still long enough to listen to the soul. The ego knows if we hear the soul calling, we will never go back to the ego. Egos are worried of losing control.

All of the major religions that I have studied have the same truths: Joy, love and peace. The ego says that we will have joy, love and peace tomorrow or yesterday but never today.

Do the following statements sound familiar? "If only I had done X, then I would have (love, joy, peace.) Or, if I do this, then tomorrow, I will have (love, joy peace.)"

The ego knows the only place to find love, joy or peace is through the soul. The only way to the soul is to force the mind to stay quiet long enough to hear it. This is why all of the great teachers tell us that we must meditate in order to quiet our minds. And the ego will never allow it. Why? Because, as soon as we understand this fact, who would want an ego?

Who among us has attempted to meditate in some way and later, given up because you could not keep quiet long enough?

---

*Live fully in the present moment and learn to listen to the thinker in you.*

---

From there, you begin to take back control of the mind, and use it for the tool it was meant to be, turning it on and off as needed.

Here is an example of how some people create an environment where they can live in the present and be fully alive. Think of people who love to engage in dangerous activities such as mountain climbing, car racing, downhill skiing, etc. They may not be aware of it, but these activities force them to live completely in the present. Their intensively alive state is free of time, free of problems, free of thinking, and free of the ego. If they do not stay in this state of mind, it could very well mean death for them. This reality forces them into the present, and frees them from the future or the past.

You can enter this state now. With practice, you can live in this state and find a joy to life. You do not have to climb Mt. Everest either.

Begin by stepping back and unemotionally listening to your mind (and your ego) as you go through your day. Be your **Self**. However, step back to watch the **thinker** in you. You will soon begin to see patterns in your reactions of thought. Suddenly, you will notice your thinking is processed by the ego and tied to the past or the future, not to the present. Try to listen and watch without judgment. Notice what emotions your thoughts bring up and then act according to the present.

You need not worry about tomorrow. Tomorrow will take care of itself as you live fully today. Yesterday is gone and it matters only to your ego. Let yesterday go. There is way too much to live for today.

We have talked about the ego a great deal. I like to give my ego a name and have found this works for me. Maybe, you will find it works for you to do the same.

## **Gremlins**

It is a wonder we can function at all. Each of us has multiple personality types all crying for attention. Most of us think one way, work another, and feel in a personality style different from either working or thinking styles. And you question why you are sometimes confused!

On top of all that, there is our ego to deal with. Our ego has a representative that might be considered a lobbyist. Like one of those people always talking to you, promoting their agenda, and trying to convince you to do it their way. I call this little guy my Gremlin, and he is always trying to sit up on my shoulder and whisper in my ear.

It is very important to know about Gremlins. They hate change. (Change hurts) They do not like to take chances. (Bruised egos) No new relationships, no stepping out on a limb, no way! They love comfort, and feed on the negative emotions we all have within us.

Have you ever heard your Gremlin whisper to you?

"You can't do that, you don't have enough experience." (No confidence)

"Wait until tomorrow to finish this, you are tired and need some rest. Besides, who is going to notice?" (Procrastination)

"You can't join them, they are better (smarter, prettier, richer) than you." (Jealousy)

We each have a Gremlin who can also be called our ego. Our Gremlin's voice is sometimes difficult to differentiate from our spirit voice or intuition. Here are some ways to learn this:

Gremlins tend to be negative and harmful. Intuition is positive and is looking out for your Self.

Gremlins are mind based and send false messages to your feelings. Intuition is heart based.

Gremlins preach procrastination. Intuition doesn't lie, and says do it now.

Gremlins hate change of status quo and will tell you anything to stop change. Intuition leads you down your chosen path, no matter where that path might go.

Make it a practice to listen closely for your gremlin. Gremlins are impossible to eliminate. They can be exposed, driven into a corner and controlled. Give your Gremlin a name and begin to recognize that you have the power to control.

---

*Learn to trust your intuition.*

---

This is the Universe giving the assistance you require.

To some this may be a little out in left field. Give it a try. The worst that can happen is someone overhears you talking to yourself. "Hey Gremlin! I see you. Get back in your corner and stay there. I have no time or patience for your shenanigans today."

Begin now. Controlling your Gremlin is to take control of you.

One way to do this is to carve time and space for yourself.

## **Where Is Your Place?**

I have a space to go. This space is my office, my haven, my place to be me and for me to do my thing. Within me are my library, music, journals, and pictures.

In this space, I find that my productivity is much higher than anywhere else. It is almost as if the surroundings contribute to my energy and creativity.

Look around you at your surroundings. Are you comfortable? Do you have at your disposal the tools you need and require to do your best? Do you have a space to go specifically for you?

I suggest that you carve one out wherever you can. Make sure everyone knows it is yours, (as much as you can,) and go there when you need to do so.

---

*Remember this: if you do not take care of yourself, no one else will.*

---

This is your primary responsibility in life. It is completely up to you to make absolutely sure you are all you can be.

I can hear it now. "What about my kids? What about my spouse? Don't they deserve my attention first? Aren't I supposed to take care of them?

You can certainly choose to give your Self completely to someone else. Ask your Self this question. Do you think you

*Be Do Have*

as a person would be better for someone else if you were whole yourself – first?

If you don't take care of you, and you give your energy to others all the time, do not be surprised when you find yourself emotionally, physically and mentally bankrupt. If you do not take the time to re-supply and call back the energy you give away, you will feel something is missing.

Please begin to think of a place just for you. It could be a closet, a corner in a room, or a room to Your Self. Find a curtain or a panel wall or a Chinese partition – whatever it takes.

Make that space yours. Nurture your soul there, do your meditation, your exercises, write your journal and listen to your inner voice. You will find more energy, strength, love and peace in your life.

You will have a place to begin the process to define who you really are. Knowing your values, defining success for you, listening for your Gremlin and your intuition are all very important.

As you work through this process, do not be surprised if you feel changes are required in your life. Change affects people differently.

## **Change Is Good**

My life has been one big change. For instance, although my wife and I have been married over 18 years, we have never lived in any one place longer than 2.5 years.

I know when changes are coming. I feel restless, a mild depression as if something were wrong, and a strong sense of - do something. If the universe is giving a signal, there is a reason behind it. Sometimes I can see the reason clearly, but most times not much makes sense until I can look back and understand all that happened.

Sometimes it takes a great leap of faith to do this.

*You must have faith in yourself and your subconscious feelings and intuition.*

There are many more times where I have wished I HAD acted on my intuition than times I was proved wrong by listening to that little voice.

Do you get these feelings and ignore them like I used to? Remember Gremlins hate change. He/she will go to any lengths to convince you that you are much better off where you are. Your Gremlin invented procrastination and is the keeper of all excuses.

*Control your Gremlin or your Gremlin will hold*

*you back all your life.*

---

You may find yourself in a place which seems like you are swimming in jello, in slow motion, not getting anywhere, and wondering why you are bothering. Stop swimming and look around you.

Listen closely to your inner voice, ignore the Gremlin. Make a change in your life, your attitude, your outlook, your job, your relationships, goals, or anything else to free your spirit to FLY instead of forcing it to swim in jello.

One last comment on change is this. When you do decide to change, you have a direction, a new goal. Although this new goal may, and often will, temporarily add to your workload, you will find an added reservoir of energy to deal with it. In fact, you will find an increased enthusiasm for life, an excitement of new possibilities and challenges to come.

This is what makes life worth living.

What else can be done to be who you are? Do you think the people around you affect your life?

## **Attraction – A Way Of Life**
### **What types of people are in your life?**

Take an inventory this week, and look hard at those with whom you associate. Isn't it difficult enough to maintain your own perspective on attitudes, optimism, goals, and generally have a positive outlook without having to struggle against other negatives surrounding you?

Are there people in your life who do not belong? You need to remove them from your life. Not in an ugly way, but people are a huge influence.

How do we find people we do want to be around?

We attract them to us by who we are.

We must, on a daily basis, constantly work on our own values, attitudes and thoughts, in order to attract into our lives those folks who will enrich and add to our own experience.

Attraction is not an easy thing. However, neither is success, no matter how you define it.

Many of the topics we have covered before must be incorporated into our lives to make us attractive to those who we wish to come to us. Goals, listening, passion, honesty, integrity, beliefs, thoughts and work habits all play a part. The great thing is we all have the ability to make this work for us.

I have also found as you work to make yourself attractive, the resulting YOU is worth all the effort. All it requires is the determination to do it.

You might have a question about the end result from this work. When we know who we are, and we live according to our values, are we then perfect?

## **How Good Do We Have To Be?**

The following is from the book "How Good Do We Have To Be?" written by Harold S. Kushner.

When we do something wrong, because we are human and our choices are so complicated and temptation so strong, we do not lose our humanity. However, we do lose our integrity, our sense of wholeness, of being the same person all the time. We create a situation where part of us, our good self, is at war with another part of us, our weak and selfish side. We lose the focus, the singleness of purpose, which enables us to do the things important to us. That is when we need the religious gift of atonement and forgiveness (making our split selves *at one*). But, should we ever conclude that there is no point in trying to be good enough that is when we lose everything. Being human can never mean being perfect, but it should always mean struggling to be as good as we can and never letting our failures be a reason for giving up the struggle.

Isn't this an interesting thought? All of us are imperfect. We all will make mistakes, commit errors, hurt others, and fail. This is inevitable and part of our individual paths to knowledge, wisdom and growth.

The question is – what do we do with these failures? Where do they go inside us?

We all know people who carry around guilt and use it as a weapon. We know people who attempt to blame everyone else for their self-made challenges.

A valuable lesson to learn is the trick of looking closely at things that go wrong for the gifts they bring. Sometimes these gifts are well hidden and we must dig deep to find them. Allow yourself the freedom to release the wrongness in whatever way works for you. Ask forgiveness of your Self, others who are affected and from God, the Universe or whatever you might call the source of all our power. This forgiveness allows us to move on without the burdens so heavy to carry and add up so quickly to create an overwhelming load.

This applies to wrongs done to others as well as to ourselves. As humans, we are not perfect and do not want to be. Life is however, perfect as it is.

And never stop trying. We all know and have heard many times there are only two ways to live. You are either dying or growing. There is no standing still in life. This is your choice.

So then – how good do we have to be?

Are you being you? That is how good you need to be.

To this point you have been given tools to help you be who you are. This is a lifelong process. In the beginning we stated that being is dynamic, and always changing to meet the present.

Part of being who you are is doing what you love.

*How could you possibly be who you are if you are not doing what you love?*

## **Be Who You Are - Final Thoughts**

The exercises and thoughts I have shared with you consist of tools and ideas to build something you can stand on. We call it a personal foundation. Just like a skyscraper, each of us must have a strong foundation to build upon. If the foundation is not strong, the whole structure is weak.

This is not a quick and easy process. All of us will always be strengthening our Self. We will tweak our values. We will change our definitions of success as goals are reached and priorities change in our lives.

This is a great start for what is to come. Doing the exercises, and giving consideration to the ideas presented here will help you move forward on your own path of personal growth and awareness.

---

*Personal growth and awareness allows you to be you and to be proud of who you are.*

---

Next - Do what you love.

# Do

In 1960, a researcher interviewed 1500 business-school students and classified them in two categories: those who were in it for the money - 1245 of them - and those who were going to use the degree to do something they cared deeply about - the other 255 people. Twenty years later, the researcher checked on the graduates and found that 101 of them were millionaires - and all but one of those millionaires came from the 255 people who had pursued what they loved to do!

## **Do What You Love**

Ask your Self this question. Am I passionate about my life or am I passing my life?

Do what you love is the second ingredient of the *BeDoHave* formula. As we work on, and allow our Selfs to be natural we begin to feel more at ease, less stressed and more relaxed. It is much easier to just "be" than to work at Being somebody or something we are not.

To Do what you love requires a commitment, and sometimes even a price. This price might be in lifestyle (how much money you have), or company (the people you associate with) or place. Doing what I love to do has meant many changes in my life others might not be willing to undergo. Examples are: changes in where I live, with whom I work, and my level of income. Sometimes doing what I love means earning less money than I might otherwise earn. The choice is yours to make. Thankfully, we all have a choice.

In these pages you will learn how to do what you love. The lessons might be how to recognize what you love to do, or how to get the most benefit from what you have decided to do.

Realize there are times when you must compromise as you work toward something in your life. How many actors and actresses are waiting tables while pursuing their dream?

Always remember you have the freedom to choose what you want to do.

*Be Do Have*

---

*Y**ou have the ability to take actions on a daily basis to create your future.*

---

Work on discovering what it is you want to do, then work on doing it!

## **Jump Out Of Bed!**

A young man of 28 who came to me for coaching had been laid off.

He was understandably upset, and a bit lost. He had been employed by a company for the last ten years, since he was eighteen, only taking time off to attend college for a bachelor's degree in the trade in which he worked.

The dismissal was a complete surprise and shock to say the least. There had been no prior warnings and he had believed he was contributing to the overall health and benefit of the company.

Just to enable you to see the whole picture, he had just bought a house, was paying for a truck and his savings were – well can we say they were not!

He wanted help figuring out what to do. He had never looked for a job and had no clue where to start.

The first question I asked him was: What do you want to do? To help him find out, he completed the following exercises.

*Be Do Have*

Go to http://www.ncsu.edu/careerkey/you/ and take the free evaluation.

Circle or answer the following statements.

1) Circle your ideal work environment—large corporation, small business, government agency or nonprofit organization.
2) Circle your ideal location—urban, suburban or rural.
3) List your three most useful job skills and circle which is your strongest.

_____

_____

4) Do you want to work with people, data or things?
5) Do you want to work with others or work alone?
6) Do you enjoy new projects or prefer following a regular routine?
7) List some of the main career areas which might interest you.

_____

_____

_____

_____

8) List your favorite leisure time activities.

_____

_____

_____

*Be Do Have*

> 9) What kind of reward is most important to you in a job—money, security, creative authority, etc?
> _____
>
> What do the answers above tell you?
> _____
> _____
> _____

It turns out that this young man, who has a BS in Construction Management, and who has spent the last ten years of his life working in that profession has realized that he would love to be the photographer for the San Diego Chargers!

He is very clear about his wants. He can (and has) explained why he wants this, how he is going to get it and how long it will take him. He is excited and cannot wait to get out of bed in the morning!

He is addressing his financial concerns to trim expenses and enable pursuit of his goal.

When asked why he never did it before, he said, "I did not know I could"!

And finally we come to my point. Are you doing what you want to do?

Life was not meant for us to work to get by. Nor were we meant to work just to put bread on the table.

*L*ife *was meant to do the things that excite you, things that make you spring out of bed in the morning, and things that make the days fly by. When you are doing this, everything else will fall into place.*

Find the answers to the above questions. Take the free survey.

Here's hoping you jump out of bed in the morning and do not lie in bed waiting and hoping for change to come to you.

## Cricket In The Wall
### Waiting and Hoping

There is a cricket in my wall. It is a very energetic cricket, continuously chirping to let me know he is there. The cricket has been at this for hours now. I wonder if he is tired. I also wonder if there are any other crickets in my wall. Knowing my two sons, it is highly likely that they brought the cricket inside the house and set it down and forgot about it. In which case the cricket can make all the noise it wants, and no other cricket will ever hear him.

Will the cricket continue trying to find other crickets by his chirping? Does he have faith that another cricket will somehow make it inside the house? Is the cricket going to keep on making the noise if it doesn't get anything to eat or drink until it dies in the wall?

What about you? Are you doing something over and over that is not working? Maybe you are in a wall! Have you considered other options for doing what you are doing?

For instance, are you happy doing the work you do? If you are, congratulations! If not, how long are you going to drag your Self to work every day before you look at other options?

The difference between the cricket in my wall and you in your situation – is that the cricket will most likely die in the wall because he doesn't have the power of reasoning to understand his options. You have this power. You were also given the power of choice. Every day you can make decisions that change everything. Every minute is a brand new chance with new choices to make.

Are you making your choices? Or are you, like the cricket, hoping something happens?

---

*What would you do differently if you were given the chance?*

---

What would you change now if you were able to wave a magic wand and start from scratch? No ties, no burdens, no limits, no memories, and no past. What would your life look like?

If the answer that comes to your mind is different than what you are doing, you need to ask your Self…why? Why are you not doing what you want? Is it because of someone else? I think the ultimate test is to close your eyes and place your Self on your deathbed. (Fun, huh?) Now, look back at your life as you are currently living it. What do you think? Have you lived completely? Or will you wish you had done it differently; been bolder, given more to others, tried harder, or done more?

I must admit to a certain amount of holding back on dreams and goals because of our two boys. However, as my life progresses, I realize there is no reason for this. There is so much we want to do! Yet as we look back on our lives, there is great satisfaction realizing that we have almost always done exactly what we wanted.

Many people find a job, call it a career and make a living at it. However, they might begrudge every minute of it, sometimes going so far as using the job as a reason for playing the martyr to friends and family.

If this is the case for you, find something else to do! Decide today to find your calling, no matter how long it takes. With the many opportunities today in every field imaginable, somewhere, something is calling to you.

A very important step to this process is to talk to those closest to you about your wants. I find some of my clients have kept their wants and needs bottled up inside them all of their life. They had already decided for the other person that there was no interest in whatever it was they themselves wanted to do. How absurd! How can we possibly know what someone else wants? Wouldn't it be tragic to spend your life working a job you despise in the city for 40 years, because you thought your partner liked it, although you wanted to live in the country and be a farmer? Then later, you found out your partner had wanted to live in the country all along?

Sure this is a bit far fetched – but you would be amazed at what I hear. My point is simply this: make an attempt today to start a brand new page.

---

*Write your life story the way YOU want it.*

---

If there are others in your life to be involved, have them do the same exercise. Then compare what each of you has written. If what you have written is what you are living, then congratulations. You are one of the few.

However, if your life story sounds like someone completely different, then you are living a life of conflict. Here is the good news. Your life is your life. No one can take that away from you. You are not indentured. You are not a slave. You are free to go, do, and be whomever you wish. Ben Franklin in the book of Poor Richard said, "Better is a little with content than much with contention."

---

*It might not be easy, but it sure might be worth it.*

---

I coach people daily who are changing their lives. As we move into this new century there are so many things to be grateful for, and so many things open to us. We owe it to all the people who went before us and to those who gave us this opportunity to take advantage of it…Today.

## **Sometimes Changes Are Forced!**

Changes can be very challenging. Sometimes we question our choice of career, the place where we live, and even our choice of life partners and friends.

This is normal. I believe the cause of this is your Self, otherwise known as your Soul. From the time we were born into the world, our egos have been hard at work to help identify who we are in relation to the physical world, usually through acquiring things, like money, power and position. However, there are many who believe that we were placed here, or we chose to come here, for a reason. Maybe that reason was to learn something, to teach something, or to help someone. Many of the teachings say we are here to serve.

There comes a time in our lives, sometimes as young as 30, and sometimes much later, when our Self wants to be heard.

---

*The Self knows what its mission is and begins to nudge you, in subtle ways, to discover that mission.*

---

This nudging can be felt as a longing for something different and new without having any specific target - just a feeling of 'something needs to happen.' If this call is not heeded, the nudging can turn into something more powerful like disease or accidents structured to allow you to take the time to figure it out.

When the nudging begins, a common response is fear. We fear the unknown. Why in the world would someone be unhappy with a high paying job, or a wonderful family, or a great lifestyle? The fear is: If I change this, what will happen?

My answer to this dilemma is to address the challenge differently than you might have been trained to do. If you are feeling this nudge, be it an indifference or boredom to your job, a restlessness and feeling of there has to be something more, I have a suggestion on how to handle it.

> Carve out some time in your daily activities; 15 minutes of quiet time will be plenty for this exercise.
>
> 1. Begin by dreaming big! What would you do if you could do anything you wanted to do; if there were no obstacles whatsoever?
>
>    _____
>    _____
>
> 2. Complete the following sentence at least three times. I'll be successful when I...(You should already have done this)
>
>    _____
>    _____
>
> 3. What are the four values in your life that pull you forward as defined earlier?
>
>    _____  _____
>    _____  _____

Put these answers all together and see what emerges. What does the combination of your dreams, values and success definitions reveal to you? How could you put a plan in action that would attract your dream to you?

*If you take a step towards your dream, your dream will absolutely come to you!*

Here are nine powerful questions for you to answer. The answers to these questions would tell me an incredible amount of information about you. These answers will also allow you a very revealing look at your Self.

1. What are you going to do today to move forward along the path you have chosen?
   _____
   _____

2. Where do you want to be in five years?
   Everybody has a plan. Either you make your own or you work someone else's plan.
   _____
   _____

3. What are you wasting your time with?
   _____
   _____

4. What is holding you back the most? Eliminate it!
   _____

5. What will your legacy be?
   What are you doing that will provide value (not just monetary) for future generations?
   _____
   _____

6. Whose life are you living?
   _____

7. What gets you out of bed every day?
   _____
   _____

8. What is the dream you have given up on?
   _____
   _____
   _____

9. What are you waiting for?
   _____
   _____
   _____

Answer these questions honestly and completely, and I sincerely hope you will be profoundly affected!

## **Finding What We Love To Do?**

To begin, we need to know what we are *not* passionate about. How about what you do now? Do you 'jump out of bed' each day, anticipating what is to come? At the end of the working day, do you find your Self not wanting to quit?

> List a few things that you might have done or that you see others do that definitely turn you off! This will give a good indication of where not to go.
>
> 1. _____
>    _____
>    _____
>    _____
> 2. _____
>    _____
>    _____
> 3. _____
>    _____
>    _____
> 4. _____
>    _____
>    _____

Where do we find our passion?

> Look back in your life and find a time that you were truly excited about something. Go all the way back to school days if you need to. Did you talk in front of a group? Help with a team effort on a charitable cause? Build a fishpond in your back yard? Play a musical instrument? Are you excited about camping, landscaping, nature, wildlife, conservation, environment, politics, race relations, sports, or children? Take some time and write a few ideas down. Then write why this stirs you like it does!
> _____
> _____
> _____
> _____
> _____
> _____
> _____
> _____

After you have a couple of ideas, you have a starting point. Now, let these ideas simmer and cook for a while. The unconscious mind works in wonderful and mysterious ways.

*If you are truly passionate about something – enough to really stir you - your subconscious will find a way to make it work.*

Look for opportunities in strange places. Keep a journal of your thoughts and look for patterns that will illuminate your path. Excitement comes as you realize that your future, like everything else, is built one step at a time, not all at once in a blinding flash. You can also get excited about the fact that you *can* choose your path!

Now look at your lifestyle. Lifestyle ties into passion very closely, because many of us are living a lifestyle that controls what we do. For us to live our passion, we must take control of our lifestyle and ensure it is in step with our passion - financially, physically and emotionally.

I know a couple living in Maine who recently created a lot of excitement in their lives. (I am a wee bit envious!) They have decided to make a change since the kids are gone, and the weather there is a little too extreme. The husband closed a long-standing professional practice; they've sold their house, and are making preparations to move to a place they have always enjoyed.

They have decided to do something completely different, something they have dreamed about. They are full of excitement and passion! Scary? Maybe. Fun? You bet! Will it work? What does it matter? (Of course it will!)

Ask your Self this question: Am I passionate about my life? Or does life seem to be passing me by?

How much time do you spend thinking about what your passion is? Are you truly passionate about your life, your home, your work? If not, why not? These are not easy questions to answer, but if you will begin today to discover what it is you love to do, (whether you get paid or not!) then you will find a wonderful world waiting for you!

*Be Do Have*

For many of us, this question of passion has never been asked! As adults, who encourages us to think seriously about our values, our priorities, our interests and our dreams? We are reminded daily of our many responsibilities, but not of our greatest responsibility: to create the life we really want, or were meant to live.

Another challenge is that old "Gremlin" and his attitude toward change! A choice to choose passion may mean saying "No!" to family, friends or tradition. It might even mean walking away from a familiar community, safety or financial security (like your job of 20 years!) It may mean disappointing people you care about, people who love you with all their hearts.

Because of this, many of us procrastinate and avoid the subject altogether: instead, we go to work and would rather be home. We "behave ourselves," and wonder why as a society we are depressed, angry and frustrated. We watch TV and ask why life can't be like that! Do you see why some of us over-eat or smoke or drink, as well as abuse ourselves - and each other - in so many ways?

As an adult, the most important question you will ever ask your Self is: What do I really, really want to do with my life? If you have not made a start on this question, stop now. Spend five or ten minutes to write in your journal. If you could do anything in the world, what would it be?

If you don't answer that question, do you think you will ever fulfill your potential or live the life you truly want, or were meant to live?

This is not some optional or casual question to ponder "later." It is not something to put off until things get easier and you have more time, or more money, or a better situation. It is THE question of on adult life. What do you really, really want to do with this incredible gift you have? How do you want to live?

## **Five Magic Words**

Think for a moment about your Self. Is there something that you would like to have, somewhere you would like to go, or something you would like to do? What is holding you back?

I can probably guess at the possible answers…"Not enough money." "Not enough time." "I couldn't do that!"

At the risk of going out on a limb, may I suggest the only thing holding you back from doing what you would like…is you!

Every one of us was born with the power to change our lives. All of us have seen seemingly ordinary people become superheroes. Why is this? Something happens in their lives that makes them suspend belief long enough to act unconsciously. When this happens, they are able to access this power and perform extraordinary feats.

Remember, our minds are a recording device. We store away everything we read, see, hear, or otherwise, experience in our lives from before we come into the world. During this time, we also form opinions with the use of this information and from the influences of others. From opinions and beliefs, come habits. Habits then become our life - just day after day habits!

Have you ever tried to break a habit? It's not easy! That is because a habit is much easier to do than NOT do.

---
*To change a habit means you have to change your belief!*
---

The best way to break an old habit is to replace it with a new one. I'll provide a worksheet for this soon.

Here is an old story to make the point. A newly married man noticed that each time his new wife cooked a roast beef; she cut off the ends of the roast. Finally, one day, he asked her why she cut the ends each time. She told him her mother had always cut the ends of the roast and had taught her to do the same. He was intrigued with the story. The next time the newlyweds visited her parents, he took the opportunity to ask his wife's mother why she cut the ends of the roast. His wife's mother said, "I cut the ends off the roast because my mother always did".

Well, of course the next time they visited grandmother, he had to ask her the same question. "Grandmother, your granddaughter is a great cook, but she always cuts the ends off the roast. She says her mother did it that way and her mother said you always did it too. I was curious why? "Grandmother said, "I cut the ends of my roast beef off so it would fit in the pan!"

Now, we are back where we started. If there is something you truly want in your life, you can get it. The very first step is to change your belief. Believe that it is possible. One of the most powerful things you can do for someone is to allow them the freedom to change their belief and their thinking process.

This can be as simple as the statement - What I want for you is...

These five magic words allow you to believe in possibilities. They begin the process necessary to create it. Your mind will take that information in and bounce it around for a while. Your mind might, with a bit of help from your Self, begin to change your belief a thing is impossible, and begin to believe that it is possible...even reachable. As soon as your intentions to the Universal Power are clear, this Power has no choice but to help you by presenting opportunities for you. (You do have to be clear enough to see the opportunities and you must act!)

Think of all you can do! What is it you would truly love to do?

I want that for you!

Does that mean you must change? Probably. Will it be for the better? Absolutely! Will it hurt? Well...

Change can hurt. Growth almost always is painful. In my mind, change means growth; therefore, I believe change is good!

# **Habits**

We are creatures of our habits. I do the same things most every morning. After I am up, (pretty much at the same time each morning,) I head directly to the shower. I dress according to my morning schedule, then head for the kitchen for a big glass of water and down to the office and my computer. Most days, all of this is done without much thinking because it is habit.

Most of us have routines that we use on a consistent basis. It has been said that the majority of mankind goes through their whole life virtually asleep! We live on auto-pilot, going from one ingrained habit to another. Then we wonder why our lives stay the same! Have you heard this saying: "Insanity is doing the same thing over and over and expecting different results."

It usually takes 21 days to begin a new habit. Some say it takes up to six weeks. There is good news here.

*By beginning new habits, we can replace old ones that no longer serve us.*

Within each of us is an ego who has spent a lifetime building a lifestyle that will not end without a fight. Have you tried drastic change lately? It is so easy to declare you are going to lose weight, start an exercise program, change your diet, take more time off, or any number of other scenarios we all have seen. However, when it comes down to actually putting these declarations into practice and forming

*Be Do Have*

new habits, watch out! Your ego and your old habits will fight you tooth and nail! Unfortunately, they usually win.

Many people lose this battle before they get started. The battle for positive personal change is lost in the mind, in the thoughts. The most difficult part of change is feelings. Emotions are a powerful ally of our ego and under its complete control. The little gremlin sits on your shoulder whispering in your ear when you want to do something different. "You can't do that," he whispers. "People will make fun of you and laugh at you behind your back," he says. "You will fail miserably," he gleefully shouts. Do you hear these voices? Do you get these feelings?

I have learned that the solution to this problem lies in my thoughts. If I am willing to change my thinking, I can change my feelings. If I change my feelings, I can change my actions. And changing my actions, based on good thinking, changes my life.

Here is why:

I can control my thoughts.
My feelings come from my thoughts.
I can control my feelings by controlling my thoughts.

---

*To enable each of us to reach the goals and dreams we harbor, we must take action.*

---

*Be Do Have*

The best way to take action is one step at a time. The best way to begin these steps is to make them a habit. Start with small habits.

What would happen if you picked good habits that you would like to have in your life? Make them happen by focusing on one thing at a time if need be, but make the change. You will be exercising your habit muscles, your thinking muscles; thereby beginning the process of creating a new life for Your self. You will also, by default, be replacing old habits that may not serve you any longer. Here are some examples:

1. Read non-fiction 15 minutes a day.
2. Set up a 30 - 60 minute appointment daily to play with your kids.
3. Send a virtual card, or write a note to someone you have lost contact with once a day.
4. Set aside 15 -30 minutes a day to do nothing at all.

You get the idea. Change hurts, but the pain is well worth the payment.

Here is an easy exercise to greatly improve your day, week and life. Introduce into your life ten daily habits to keep you focused. Stay clear on what you are doing and always moving forward.

There are a few rules involved.

1. Choose only those habits you want to do! This is no place for shoulds or coulds. Pick things you

like to do, things you would look forward to and feel good when you had done them.
2. Choose habits to increase your energy flow. You want to do things to add to your well-being and happiness.
3. Change your habits if necessary. If you find you are not doing what you picked, nor are happy doing them, then change your habits! Pick habits that come naturally.

Here are some ideas.
    Compliment a stranger every day.
    Spend one hour with the one you love.
    Write in your journal.
    Exercise.
    Do the one major thing on your 'to do' list.
    Place one call a day to someone you haven't talked to in a while.
    Tell the Universe for what you are grateful.

Make a list of twenty or so habits like these that appeal to you. Then circle the ten most attractive. (You can always add more if you like!) Ask your Self: What habits could I do every day that would enrich my life?

_____  _____

_____  _____

_____  _____

_____  _____

_____  _____

_____  _____

*Be Do Have*

_____        _____

_____        _____

_____        _____

_____        _____

Now do them! Make a poster or a calendar and post it in a prominent place so that you can see your new habits all the time. Then check them off every day until these become habits. If you find your Self not doing them, ask your Self why? If need be, change your habits to ones you will do!

Maybe changing your habits will require you to leave your comfort zone. We all have comfort zones. Just like this dog I once knew.

## **Comfort Zone**

There is an invisible fence made for dogs. It consists of a wire buried underground and a dog collar. The underground wire creates an electrical current in the collar as the dog approaches the places the wire is buried. The dog will begin to feel an electrical shock as it draws near and will definitely get zapped when approaching too close to the wire. Flags similar to those marking underground utilities are placed nearby so the dog can see where the wire is located.

Did you know after a while the dog will not go anywhere *near* the flags, even if the electricity is turned off?

This is the dog's *comfort zone*!

Each of us has a comfort zone and we aren't even aware of it! This zone is holding us back from living, as we would like. We have been "shocked" by life when we try something new, so we tend not to try again.

Answer me this: If we place a huge, meaty bone *outside* the invisible fence, and the dog decides it is worth the pain involved to jump through or over the wire – getting shocked in the process – will the dog go *back through the fence?*

Of course not! He is free of the boundaries of the fence!

We are just like that dog! We have fenced ourselves in by comfort levels.

*F*ind *your bone and go get it.*

Just imagine the whole new world waiting you! Yes, you might get shocked!

But then again, someone may have turned the fence off!

## **Change**

There are lots of reasons we have difficulty breaking out of our comfort zones. One big reason would be because it causes us to leave our comfort zone and that means we must change! Let's talk about change.

First, there is your Gremlin! We talked about our Gremlins a few chapters back. You know, the little fellow/gal sitting just behind your ear? Just sitting their minding his own business until you try to change the status quo! It is amazing how fast you can wake him up!

Let's say you want to lose weight. That is a change, right? Your Gremlin will jump all over that! It will make suggestions such as:

"You look fine just the way you are!"
"If you do that you'll have to buy all new clothes."
"One piece of cake won't make any difference!"
"You'll just gain it back anyway!"

You see? Gremlins are sly, tricky, conniving and absolutely hate change!

Another challenge is your environment of your friends, family and associates. They like you the way you are! If you change, that means they have to change too. Now you have their Gremlin up in arms as well!

Let's say you have traditionally been somewhat of a lazy, no good, bum. Over a period of time, you realize you are a bum and decide to change. You start a business from your home, a landscaping service. You go to the bank to borrow money for equipment – "HA," they say. "You are a bum," and they'll probably never give you the money. You attempt to get your friends, family and associates to give your new service a try. "HA," they say. "You are a bum - you'll always be a bum!" Make sense? They are unable to see the new you.

When I was growing up, my family moved a lot. I attended 12 or more different schools! Somehow early on, the realization came to me every time we moved somewhere new, I could change whatever I wanted; my clothes, my hair, my habits, or my attitude. You see, no one knew any different; therefore, they accepted the 'new' me. The only person that I had to change - was me!

Therefore, the answer is simple. If you want to get out of your comfort zone, and make some sort of change in your life, it is easy. Move!

Just kidding, (although it does work.)

Here are a couple of simple tips for creating change:
1. Have a compelling reason for your change. Write it down, with the changes you want and post it where you will see it every day.
2. Don't broadcast your decision to the world. For one thing, you don't need the additional pressure of living up to your statements. Another reason is that you might change what you originally decided to do!
3. Tell your Gremlin to be quiet and all will be fine!
4. Find a mentor or a personal coach to help you. It is almost essential to have someone in your life at

times like this to support you, listen to you and help you see the "big picture" when you are in the trenches dealing with the daily struggles.

## **Major And Minor**

As we sift through the collection of treasures and junk that make up our life and take up our precious time, often we must make a decision whether to do one thing over another. You think about going, but then hesitate. Today, for instance, after you were dressed and ready to go somewhere, let's say that you realized it would be a great day to take your kid fishing with a cane pole and a picnic lunch.

Why don't you?

If you are like me, with a mortgage, insurance, food, clothes and transportation to provide, your decision is to earn an income instead of going fishing.

---

*The question is – is fishing major or minor in your life?*

---

Only you can answer that.

However, we must scrutinize *every* decision we make for major and minor. With limited time available to each of us, and the sometimes-overwhelming choices to fill every second of each day, the decisions we make can and do affect us profoundly.

One of the time consumers I am most passionate about is television. Personally, I believe that TV does more damage to people's lives than almost anything else. Don't get mad at me

– that is only my opinion! However, look at the time you spend in front of a TV and imagine using that time in a *major* project such as an exercise program, or starting a home based business, or writing a book, or taking a class.

Not only will you be learning skills that will benefit you, you will also be eliminating the garbage flowing into your brain, which you can't control! (I told you I was passionate about it!) BTW – we have not watched television for over 10 years now.

---

*L*ook at everything you do and decide – *"Is this major or minor?"*

---

Use this qualification to make choices that enrich your life, that work toward your goals and dreams, and make you feel as though your time is well spent.

Another tool to use with decisions is prioritization.

The world and our lives seem to be speeding up. One hour, one day, one week, or even one year will fly by and the next one is right there demanding attention.

Sometimes it seems as though my attention is being used up by minor things; stuff that might not be as important and useful in the overall plan.

Here is a little exercise to sort through in order to determine what is major and/or what is minor. See what deserves attention and what must take a back seat. I think this will surprise you.

First, I think we can all agree that we are here for a relatively short time and I, for one, do not believe we are here to only work. Contribute yes, but not to spend our whole lives as a machine for others. The idea then is to find out *why* we are here and do that. As soon as we are able to clearly define the reason that we are here, then it is easy to decide what is a major and what is a minor thing.

*Be Do Have*

Try this:

From the list below, place a number next to FIVE of the priorities you would have in your life IF IT WERE UP TO YOU (not how it *is* currently but how you *wish* it to be). If you had your way, what would be most important to you? Put a 1 in front of that. Second most important? Put a 2, and so on. Number only five items. If you have something that isn't on the list, add it in. These are your IDEAL priorities.

___ Health and well-being   ___ Hobbies
___ Family                  ___ Creative pursuits
___ Satisfying, well        ___ Adventure
     paying work            ___ Education
___ Friends                 ___ Recreation
___ Community service       ___ Money
___ Religious or spiritual life   ___ Other

Now, write the top five IDEAL priorities below and rank them in order of your REAL life.

_____
_____
_____

How do your top five ideal items compare to your *real* life?

_____
_____
_____

*Be Do Have*

I found this to be a fascinating exercise! If they match or closely match, congratulations, you are living the life you want. Few people can say this!

If your lists are fairly far apart, what are you going to do? I would guess you might be having challenges in your life troubling you. You might find your Self angry, upset, or otherwise emotionally troubled. Your answers to your challenges lie before you.

Your goal is to have your real life match your ideal life. Begin making decisions to advance your ideal priorities. Find a place for those priorities in your life, and your life will be so much better!

Our family uses these ideals to make sure we stay on track, accomplish the important to-dos required to meet our long term objectives, and plan our days. We also use this to integrate our business activities into our schedule.

## **Brain Dump Activity**

Purpose:
Clear your head, capture all activities, ideas, and projects into one master plan. Schedule and assign activities.

Materials:
Small sticky notes, pens, lots of blank walls or table surfaces, and pads: Cut your sticky notes in half if you don't have the small ones.

Step One:
Write down every possible activity you can think of that needs to happen for your life and business. This alone will take several days to assemble. Write each on a separate sticky note. Ideally, the task on each sticky note should be a task that can be completed in one session. For example, instead of writing a sticky note that says, "write a marketing plan," you might create ten sticky notes, one for each component of a marketing plan (market analysis, competitive assessment, gather media kits, create master advertising plan, build press list, etc.)

However, sometimes you just won't know all the components. When this happens, just write one sticky note for the major task.

Step Two:
Take all of your stickies and begin organizing them by subject matter in categories or columns on a wall or table. Create your categories or columns from your own experience. Sometimes, you won't be sure which column to put it in; make a miscellaneous column for those items.

When you're finished, review the miscellaneous items to see if any of them will fit in other columns. Remove any duplicates.

Step Three:
After you get everything in columns, go to each column and prioritize. Put the most important on the top and work down. Assign each task (put initials in the corner.) You might also note which category on each sticky note.

Then, go across the tops of all the columns and pluck the most important priorities and assign them to a day, a week or a month. Some activities will be things that you feel need to be done right away. That's normal because most of the stuff you'll think of (initially) will be the stuff that's on the top of your mind. That's fine, just put those on a "tomorrow" or "next week" sheet. Beyond a few weeks, put them in months. Don't try to figure out activities week-by-week beyond four weeks out.

Another useful idea is to take the sticky notes off the columns, which you plan to do that day and place them on a daily sheet. Just work on your daily sheet. If you begin work on another sticky note not on your daily sheet or something not on a sticky note at all, it is a good indication you are losing focus. There is a great feeling of accomplishment in physically throwing away completed sticky notes!

## **Time**

I read somewhere that time was not real; it's a man-made idea. Who invented clocks? Who invented daylight savings time? How strange. As if we could "save" something unreal like time.

Have you ever enjoyed doing something so much that you completely forgot about time? Time flies does it not? And the reverse is true – remember sitting in a classroom watching the second hand on the wall clock taking forever to go around one time?

---

*If time is real, then how can it be so different?*

---

Or maybe we should ask ourselves, what is it that makes the difference?

The difference is what we choose to do, and how we choose to think about our choice. You might not have "enough time" because you are spending your "time" doing things you do not want to do.

If you would like to see this for your Self, keep a little journal for a few days and write down everything you do. Then go back and sort your days into categories you arrange. Even if it is two simple categories such as **I like to do this…** and **I don't like to do this…**

Compare how much of your day is in each category. The more you worry about lack of time, the more of your time is probably in the "don't like" column!

So, what can we do about this challenge? Here are some suggestions.

---

First ask your Self these questions:
1. Why is my life so busy? Why have I chosen to do so much?

   _____

   _____

2. Where am I going/ what am I building with this lifestyle? Is there a future to this plan worth costing my present?

   _____

   _____

3. What might I be missing because of my lifestyle?

   _____

   _____

---

Then, when you are ready, try the following:

Throw out 50% of your projects, commitments, shoulds, goals, and tasks. If this is very difficult, faze them out over a 6-month period. I suggest the drastic way because it will create momentum for you to be able to see it through to the finale.

Warning! Your mind and ego will revolt, especially your ego because it relies on staying busy to feel important. Our egos are extremely crafty and subtly powerful. Believe it or not, you might have physical reactions from such a drastic change in lifestyle as your body and mind adapt.

Your priorities change; you might wonder who you are, and what you are doing. You might even get headaches, physically sick, confused and disoriented. Is it worth all this?

Benefits of drastically cutting back on the things you don't want to do include:

1. You will be much more in touch with your values, feelings and soul.
2. You will begin to make your own choices instead of reacting to what you perceive is coming at you.
3. You will begin to take care of your Self.
4. You will learn time is on your side!

---

*You will find it is worth it to change.*

---

*Be Do Have*

## Change Your Reality

How many times and how many ways can it be said you have complete control over your life; in any area of your life? This was recently brought home to me in a very powerful way.

I was sitting at my computer writing. My computer clock read 6:00 am, but yesterday at this time, it was light outside. Today, it is dark.

How many millions or even billions of people changed their reality yesterday by simply believing time had actually changed by one hour? Incredible. If we can change time, why can we not change anything else we want?

I tell you again – we can.

* Nothing is real.
* Life has the meaning you give it.
* You are who you say you are and your experience is what you say it is.

Think of your life as an incredible video game you are playing. Start by concentrating on keeping your character healthy to get the most from the game, which means doing the things within the game to get health points - like exercise. In this game there is also points awarded for gathering rest! Of course, there are points given for love as well. And one sure thing about video games is that you can always play again no matter what happens!

If we look at people who play video games, some like the game and have fun, some do not like the game and refuse to play. Some come back another time in a different frame of mind and find the game seems different, more challenging or rewarding.

---

*Do you see that the game never changes and it is the perception of the person playing the game that makes it seem different?*

---

Haven't we all heard the phrase, "Perception is 99% of reality?" So, change your perception - change your reality. If you can change reality by changing perception, then reality is not real; it is actually only what you make of it! Make reality whatever you want. Will it be easy? No. Is it doable? Yes. Your choice!

Simply make it a conscious choice.

## **Coping vs. Creating**

How many of us wander from day-to-day dealing with what life brings to us? There are two trains of thought to accompany this line of thinking. Coping and creating.

Coping is living in a world where reality (or life) comes rushing at you all day long. When you feel things have slowed down enough, you might think "Whew! Now, I can take a breather until the next thing happens!"

Is that you? Do you feel as though life is throwing you curve balls to swing at the best you can? Does fate have things in store for you and are you simply wading through, sort of waiting to see what is next?

In this admittedly broad category, you might have this type of thought:
If I only had…
or
If I only could…
or
When I get…
Then I'll be happy!

Have you ever said something similar?

---

*What if we had complete control over our lives? What if, instead of dealing with life as it approaches, we were able to \*create\* our own life as we go?*

---

*Be Do Have*

This is completely possible. I read a book not too long ago based on the teachings of the philosopher Epiticus who lived in 75AD. He taught this very idea 2000 years ago. Therefore, these ideas have been around a very long time.

You can be happy now (one of the keys to life!) and you can absolutely live whatever life you choose!

If you are in a stage of coping with a life, which is causing you to deal with issues that seem to come from nowhere; or if you have unwanted situations, which you have not asked for, the good news is, there is a better way.

In a nutshell: Stop Coping and Start Creating!

For instance, say you are coping with financial problems. You seem to run out of money before running out of month. This is a fairly typical situation in today's world. How do you start creating an income instead of coping with a lack of what you need or want?

It isn't rocket science. The answer is application of a step-by-step plan to *create* an answer to that with which you are *coping.*

Here are some steps you might take:

1. Keep a record of every penny your family spends in one week. I mean every penny! Look closely at what you spend your money on.
2. Develop a budget (get help if necessary) and STICK TO IT!
3. Set up a savings plan and pay it first! Before you pay a bill!

4. Look at ways to increase your earning potential. Take a class – learn more about how to increase your worth at work. Investigate outside income.
5. Look for ways to spend less money. For instance, my wife and I moved because we realized that we didn't need the size house we had – we only wanted it! Now, our payment is cut by 33% and the costs of our utilities are less. Additionally, there is much less maintenance with the new home. We put the extra money into building assets that manager to create more income!
6. Acquire and learn to use financial software like Quicken, QuickBooks or Money. These programs are wonderful tools for keeping tabs on cash flow!
7. Educate your Self about money!
   Read the following books!
   <u>Rich Dad, Poor Dad</u>
   <u>Science of Getting Rich</u>
   <u>The Richest Man in Babylon</u>

Take control of your life, and take steps to create your life. Is it easy? No. Can it be done? Yes!

When?

## **As Soon As...**

You know - as soon as I get done finishing my basement, I'll be so happy! Then, I'll be able to really get organized in my new office!

As soon as that is done – then, I'll really be happy! I won't have to move all sorts of stuff around to find my computer so I can write my newsletters in advance! Then, I'll be so happy – as soon as blah, blah, blah!

Do you use that phrase? As soon as (ASA?)

I think that we should remove ASA completely from our vocabulary. When we use phrases such as this, are we not putting off our being satisfied today? Are we not tying our happiness to the future the minute we say ASA?

Last week, I made a list to work on for my Self. One of the top items on the list was to learn to enjoy today much more than I do. I sometimes struggle so hard to get everything done. I am the worst offender of ASA.

ASA I cut the grass, I'll play with the kids.

ASA I practice my guitar playing and singing, I'll perform in public again.

ASA I am a little more comfortable with all the speeches I have written, I will aggressively market my Self.

Hooey! Step out now and just do it! Whether it means you are to stop doing something to smell the roses (or your kid's dirty feet!) or you are to take the bull by the horns and step way out of your comfort zone; do it!

I am going to – as soon as I finish this book!

This brings us to…

## **Procrastination!**

It is probably the number one disease in our lives today. Putting off until…for whatever reason means another day gone by. Even worse are the hidden scars left by our procrastinating actions.

Every time we put off doing something we know needs to be accomplished, not only does the thing not get accomplished, but a little piece of us is torn away. You see, your Self knows, although your ego may not allow it to be heard, by not doing the thing, you have let your Self down about a promise to your Self. In other words, you are quietly telling your Self you cannot be counted on to do what you promise! The price we all pay for the accumulation of little procrastinations adds up to a lifetime of _____ (you fill in your own blank).

I think you can fill in the blank. I know what it means to me and my life, my wife and my family.

Jim Rohn, one of my favorite motivational speakers, has said "Procrastination is an infection, and unless cured becomes a disease which will rob you of your life.

I procrastinated last week and did not complete a scheduled project. The entire week, I paid because I thought about it every day (misuse and waste of energy,) felt bad because I let my Self (and maybe, someone else) down, and also felt twinges of "Hey, if I can't even get a simple thing like this done; maybe, I'm not capable of…" Procrastination is an insidious, debilitating, energy stealing, and mind-altering disease. Have you had this happen to you?

Does procrastination affect your business? What can we do about it? Here are some hints...

1. **Get organized.**
   Every morning or the evening before (whether you are a day or night person) plan your day to come. Although difficult at first, with practice comes knowledge of the time it takes to do things and you know what you can reasonably accomplish. Set small goals for your Self. Then do what you have planned. It feels great to cross something off your list every day. If possible, plan the things you think are most disagreeable first. Get them out of the way, which will free your day to do the things you like.

2. **Take the first step and the rest will follow.**
   If my wife wants me to do something, she will simply start it. For instance, she has been asking me to build a fence around the garden. Last week, I looked out the window and saw her with the posthole diggers digging a hole. The weekend before, she started digging a fishpond! Now, we have a nice pond, a fence around the garden and me begging her to not start any more projects for a while. Simply take the first step.

3. **Set your goals.**
   Yes, I know we have heard it all before. Blah, blah. It is this simple. Your mind will accomplish what you tell it to do. Putting your goals in writing and posting them, reviewing them and

then letting your subconscious know that is what you really want will work miracles in your life.

4. **Make your Self accountable.**
If you have someone holding you accountable, you will be much more likely to accomplish what you set out to do. This person should be a confidant who you can trust with your innermost thoughts and feelings. He or she should be someone who can help you unlock the questions, dreams, and hidden blocks and gently help you see where you really are – versus where you want to be. Make certain that they are someone who has no emotional, financial or any other ties to you so they can be objective in their thoughts about your future. With this confidant, you will be able to seek out and even quite possibly find your path. Work with them and let them to help you reach your goals. (This is the work I and other professional life coaches perform.) You should be able to allow this person to hold you accountable for what you need to do.

These goals you set with them will provide a powerful incentive to keep a watchful eye on that most serious of diseases - procrastination!

## **Die In This Ditch!**

What about people who have procrastinated so long that they have become stuck in a place… or, are in a place that they cannot or care not to budge out of? We have all been there.

Perhaps, you weigh more than you would like to weigh. Maybe, you have not taken the time to maintain your exercise program and you have run out of breath getting up from the couch to the fridge.

It could be more serious. For instance, over the last few years, you may have been working a job where you are miserable, and you know a change is called for, but you can't seem to figure out just how to leave.

---

*Are you going to die in this ditch? What a great, challenging phrase!*

---

When we are faced with a challenge, whether it is internally (from your Self) or externally (from a coach or a friend,) the most common thoughts are an initial rush of positive energy as you see your Self as the new you.

However, it takes no time at all for our little Gremlin to start an uproar in your mind. He will tell you it is impossible, or hard, or perhaps, he or she will try to convince you to start tomorrow, always tomorrow.

*Be Do Have*

Ask your Gremlin. Are we going to die in this ditch?

What a wonderful, highly visual stimulator!

I had to jump start my habits after getting way off track over the last few months. I had let my daily exercises slide. The date of my last journal entry was embarrassing, and I hardly remember the last time that I had practiced my guitar.

These are things I *need* for me. There is no guilt involved as I had some fairly good excuses, albeit excuses are just that. In other words, I am not berating my Self for what I have not done. Instead, I am only realizing it is time for me to get back on track.

I, for one, do not want to die in this ditch!

## **Take Action**

There are times I have easily become overwhelmed. My intentions and goals tend to lean toward the dreamer side and may, to some, seem completely unrealistic. I have found if I contemplate for too long on the final outcome of my dreams, everything comes to a standstill. I get absolutely nothing done because I think the goal impossible to achieve. The less I get done, the more I know the dream will never happen. The more I know the dream will never happen, the less motivation I have to work on my dream. It is a vicious cycle.

For example, when we bought the hull of a sailboat with the dream of sailing around the world, I clearly remember sitting in the hull with nothing in it. I had no money, no experience with building sailboats and few tools with which to work. I remember thinking to my Self, "What in the world am I doing here?" The dream almost ended right then.

Instead, I picked up a wire brush and started cleaning. Since the boat was aluminum, wire brushing made it shiny clean. I cleaned that boat for a long time. While I was cleaning, I had time to think about what I should do next and I did it. Then I thought about the next thing and the next: 18 months later, we had a finished sailboat to put in the water.

Action is the cure. There are times in everyone's life when things seem impossible; times when we really just do not see the point in doing anything else. It might be that there is too far to go, or the future is in such doubt that we wonder why we should even bother?

*Be Do Have*

---

*A*ction is the cure.

---

My family and I have a dream of owning a horse ranch on the western slope of the Colorado Rocky Mountains. We visualize the ranch in a beautiful valley with a clear cold river flowing through the middle, surrounded by high snow-covered mountains and a clear blue sky. On our ranch, we vision guest cabins where people come and stay with us. Our guests will enjoy time on the ranch with the horses and the valley and will be able to share the life we lead for a while.

As far away as that dream seemed to us, we have taken another step closer to it by purchasing 10 acres of land. We also have a house, and an acre of cleared fenced pasture. Although we are very excited, there is so much to do. We know that we need to plan, finance and build a barn. We took action and now it is beginning to happen. We are not in Colorado yet, but this is a very positive step!

The barn is designed and staked in the field. In fact, we have already cut the trees, and we will use these as the lumber to build the barn.

You too can create whatever you want. It may seem impossible at the moment. You might think it could never be true for you. If you will simply make up your mind a thing will happen and take action, you will be utterly amazed at the forces of the Universe that will come to your aid.

But, if you allow your negative thoughts to convince you such a thing is not possible, and if you believe life is not meant for you, which is exactly what will happen to you. So choose not to 'die in the ditch'.

All you have to do is to have an intention, or a goal. Next, you will need to passionately believe in it, no matter what they all say, and take action - any positive action!

## **Action Requires Consistency**

You should see our garden! Even with the hot, very dry summer we had this year, the tomatoes grew to be mouthwatering. The cantaloupes turned out to be large and juicy, and the other wonderful fresh products of our garden such as watermelons, squash, corn, and peas are attempting to overwhelm us at the table.

Why is it that all these things happened? Well, basically, we worked, sweated, toiled, and invested time and energy. Some days, we had no time and energy to spare.

Our dream was that one-day all these wonderful foods would be available to us. My wife and I talked about how good those fresh tomatoes were going to taste and look. We visualized the shape, feel and smell of large, round perfectly ripe cantaloupes. A plan was formed whereby, we would till, plant, fertilize, water, weed, wait and harvest.

I am amazed at how many people told us, "Oh, I would love to have a garden, but I just don't have the time" (knowledge, space –whatever.)

What would have happened if we had skipped any one of these steps? No garden!

Our lives and businesses are exactly the same way. You must complete each step in its own time, and wait to harvest the results.

1. Dream a dream. A life, a goal, a desire. Feel it and then visualize the dream. Hold it clearly in your mind.

2. Plan out your dream and think about the steps you'll need to take in order to make your goal come true. Know each step... when, where, and how.

3. Work your plan. Don't stray from it. Make changes as called for so you don't get off track. Give your dream or your plan some time.

4. Keep weeding! Weed out negatives, worry, and stress. These weeds will choke and kill a dream or goal.

5. Water and fertilize! Review your goals constantly. Reward progress. Become motivated by listening to tapes, reading or writing books, or going to seminars. I have learned so much from teachers like Jim Rohn, Anthony Robbins, Dr. Wayne Dyer and others.

6. Wait to harvest. There is a time to harvest. If you plant enough seeds, and do all of the steps, there will be a crop!

The beautiful part is that one seed can provide a bountiful crop!

# **Dream, Act And Maintain!**

How many times do we intend to do something and then never quite get around to doing it? It is so easy to talk about action, but it is a whole different ball game when it comes to putting your plan into practice.

Sometimes, our subconscious mind will let us instinctively know an action is needed. Then, once we think it through, and allow our conscious thoughts time to weigh in, we talk ourselves right out of a great idea.

Many times, we have already acted subconsciously. Maybe, you could use a little exercise, and you bought a little set of leg weights to wear on your ankles as soon as you started walking around the block. "I know this will be good for me," you said to your Self.

However, when it came right down to it, those weights ended up in a yard sale. Sound familiar? We have all done something like this.

The key to doing something successful, is taking positive action – action without too much thought. When you feel something or have a spontaneous thought, many times, you are being led by an inner intelligence that needs no thought process on your part.

Listen to these calls. Act! Because as we all know, actions speak louder than words.

## **Adapt as You Need, And Plow Ahead**

Winter is on the way. I can tell because the horses are getting furry; or hairy if you prefer. (Of course, the fact that I have to wear a coat is a clue as well.)

Panic has been trying to creep past my conscious thought, but as I am a well-trained, conscious thought type of person, these feelings get halted at the proverbial door. It is good to look at these types of thoughts and understand why they occur and how to make use of them.

Since February, when we moved, I have been steadily working on building a new barn in order to provide shelter for the horses and the hay they will require for the winter. At the same time, we have been clearing land so seed can be planted to allow for grass next year. My mind wants to panic because it feels that I am not far enough along. My mind wants me to go running off in a frenzy to get all this done - today!

As I write this, I can feel the pressure weighing on me. What causes this pressure? Who is it that puts these feelings inside me to cause unrest, unease and/or discomfort? I look close and sure enough, I find out that the culprit is...me! Why in the world would one part of me want the other parts of me to experience these feelings? Maybe it is an effort to get me to hurry up and finish? Maybe it is that little my Gremlin that sometimes sits on my shoulder and says negative things like: "I told you that you couldn't do it." Or, you'll hear the Gremlin ask you, "Did I not say it would be too hard?" Certainly, you'll hear, "Why don't you just give up?" Claims will come at you such as, "You don't have enough money, time, resources"... and more.

Do you have a Gremlin too? I just tell mine, "Thanks, but please shut up." I know where he is. I also know that I am doing just fine. Maybe, I am not as far along as I would like to be. Possibly, the barn will be finished and maybe, it won't.

---

*I will do my best, celebrate and I'll be grateful for the things that I complete.*

---

I will not allow my negative thoughts or my gremlin to affect my thinking, mood, or my outlook on life. I control my thoughts, and by doing so I control my feelings; and, like the horses, I adapt. You should see the hair that I am grow-ing! (Just kidding!)

I have called for help in areas that are not my strengths to speed the process up a little. I have changed my schedule to allow for a bit more time spent here at the ranch. Lastly, I have bought a pair of very warm coveralls to be ready for old man winter.

## **Maintain It!**

Hopefully, you are beginning to understand what it is you love to do, and act on your beliefs. Realize, as in anything you have, you require maintenance to keep everything in top condition.

A few years ago (or more,) my wife and I enjoyed a life as captain and crew on a luxury motor yacht. The owner of the yacht had invested around a million dollars in his new toy.

After eighteen months of managing the yacht as a business, we realized a basic fact of life, which remains with me today. To properly maintain and upkeep his investment in the proper manner required a constant flow of time and finances.

Pretty simple isn't it? If you have something you want to keep looking its best, operating at peak performance, and increasing in value, then you must maintain it!

Let's look at some examples of how that applies to us!

Answer each of these questions honestly (on paper even) and see if you are satisfied with your answers.

1. What is your maintenance plan for your body? Is it in peak performance in case it is called upon to carry a heavy load? Are you planning on keeping your body a long time? Do you check it regularly? Look for wear and tear and replace or refurbish as necessary? Take it out for a test spin?

2. How about your mind? Do you feed it regularly the best diet that you possibly can or do you just fill it with junk? Do you get your best use from your body by exercising it regularly?

3. What is your maintenance plan for your children? Are you pumping them full of love so important to their growth? Do you fertilize and nurture yourself with the proper balance of mind, soul and body foods?

4. Follow the same line of thought with each of these: Friends, family, and work.

From my own experience, I realize it is so much more exciting to look to the future and onward toward new things. In our throwaway society, we are accustomed to simply buying a new gadget as soon as the one we have begins to break down – such as: cars, lawnmowers and appliances. Broken? Too expensive to fix? Buy a new one.

It is incredibly difficult to buy a new body, mind or child.

Take the time to incorporate into your busy life a plan for maintenance. In the long haul, you'll be glad you did.

## **<u>Now Let Go!</u>**

As we work harder to bring us closer to our dreams, we might become discouraged at the rate of our progress. There is a tool for dealing with this.

Have you ever noticed the harder you try to do something, the more difficult it can become? The more effort invested in solving a challenge or a problem, the worse the problem becomes, or at best it will frustrate you more than it will solve the problem?

Try letting go of it instead.

When something or someone takes some action that might appear to be directed at you, instead of taking it personally, realize that any action taken by others does not require a response from you. Not only does it not require a response from you, you have the wonderful ability to choose what you do - if you do anything at all!

So let it go.

The same principle applies to a challenge, a problem or even a goal. You may be facing something in your life that is highly frustrating, emotionally charged, and it may be causing havoc in you and your surroundings. If you think about it, how can an inanimate idea cause an emotion in you? It can't.

*Be Do Have*

---

*Y*ou *cause the emotion in you, not the idea, not the goal, not the challenge.*

---

Let it go.

Letting go is probably the hardest lesson I have ever tried to learn. Letting go is also the most powerful lesson I have ever tried to learn, and has brought the most rewards.

So how does one let go?

The first thought is that letting go means no judgment. If something happens in my life that seems to be directed at me either by someone else or not, then my challenge is not to place blame for what has happened. After all, hasn't it already happened? What good will it do me or anyone else to be angry, upset, or hurt over something in the past? My ego might feel better, but my soul? No - I don't believe so.

Another way to let go is to be proactive. If something happens you are not particularly pleased about, look deeply into your own feelings for the cause of this emotion. It is very likely there is something within you, which could use a little attention. Let go of the emotion and take action on you!

Letting go is not always about pain. Letting go can certainly be used for future events as well.

*Be Do Have*

*Worry is a worthless emotion tied to a future event that will more than likely never come to pass.*

Even if the thing you fear did happen, the negative emotion worry, in this case, certainly would make not one iota difference in the outcome!

Therefore, we can also let go of the future. If you have a goal, or a dream, do your best to make it a reality and let the outcome go! Let the Universe do its part without your interference. You might even get more than you asked for! (Look at the pictures of our horse farm for proof! http://www.highcountrystables.com)

Try letting go anytime you feel a negative emotion such as fear, anger, jealousy, or greed. Just catch it and say to your Self, "Self, let it go!"

Try letting go of your future. Say to your Self, "Self, I am doing my best so let go!"

You'll be glad you did.

*Be Do Have*

# **Want Money? You Got It!**

One of my favorite quotes of all time came from Yoda – a Jedi master in the movie *Star Wars* - "*Try not. Do or do not. There is no try.*"

I don't know who wrote these lines for Yoda in the Star Wars movie, but they are extremely powerful.

When we use phrases such as "I'll try," "Maybe, I can do it," "I think I can," or… "I'll give it a shot," we begin the task at a disadvantage.

*Our minds are what make things happen and it is a very simple process.*

If you will learn the process and commit to practicing the steps, your dreams will become a reality that much sooner.

First, there is thought. Even before an idea, a program, an opportunity, a job, a task, or anything else that you might be able to name, first comes a thought! The idea or thought first has to originate in a person's mind. The next step is either spoken or written. We are committing or broadcasting our thought to the world and changing it from high-speed vibrational thoughts into a slower written or spoken speed. After this thought has been altered in this manner it becomes matter. Now, this thought can be made tangible by action! Do it! Make it happen! Do you see?

*Be Do Have*

Now back to the quote. If you think, "I'll try," that is what will be communicated to the world. "I will try to do it," means the only thing that the universe has to do is to try. You see, you have control over what is to happen. If you want something bad enough, the universe has no choice but to give it to you! However you must be very clear!

How about this thought: "I want more money!" What does the universe give you when you think and speak or write this wish? It gives you exactly what you request! You now will want more money!

The next time you think, say, or write anything at all, be very conscious of what terms you use. Remember the universe must find a way to give you exactly what you request!

Here are some common ones I hear:

"I'm tired," "I need more money," or even, "I'm having a bad day."

And the universe's response will be, "You've got it!"

Interesting, don't you think?

## **Limiting Beliefs**

Not only the way you communicate, but also the way you believe is crucial to doing what you love.

How about:
"Nobody really wants to read my newsletter/book/writings?"
or – "I do not have enough time for all this."
or – "I never seem to have enough money."

How do we approach this challenge?

We must change our beliefs.

You mean change my mind? Alter my thinking? I can't do that. This is a perfect example of a limiting belief.

Do you see how the thought producing systems work?

*D*efine your limiting beliefs.

This will take some work. They are insidious, hiding under every nook and cranny.

> What belief is doing your Self harm? List every one you can think of at this time.
>
> (Example) No one would pay to hear me speak.
>
> 1. _____
>
> 2. _____
>
> 3. _____
>
> 4. _____
>
> 5. _____

Then deliberately, forcefully and methodically begin to *change your mind.*

Change your beliefs to whatever you want! You can do this.

*Be Do Have*

> Write a statement affirming the changes, which you want to make in each of your limiting beliefs.
>
> (Example) People of all ages and backgrounds easily recognize the power and passion in my message and willingly give good value to hear me express my thoughts.
>
> 1. _____
>
> 2. _____
>
> 3. _____
>
> 4. _____
>
> 5. _____

Watch out for the return of the limiting beliefs, because they will be back. But now you are ready for them!

## **Dream Big**

In my life, it seems I have always had these large dreams, which I must turn into reality. Remember the dream with the ranch in the Rocky Mountains, the horses, and the lifestyle?

Now, this vision obviously cannot happen overnight. But it will happen...Unless we alter our goals along the way! Here are a few steps you can take to turn dreams into reality:

1. **Dream.**
   Then make your dream real. How? Write it down on paper! Tell others about your dream. Describe it and feel it! Remember, everything that is; first, began as a thought. Thought is the pot from which the world is made. The computer that I used today...first began as a dream.

2. **Believe.**
   When you believe something – then it is no longer a dream...it is simply a reality. Why? Because we have stated that we believe in our dream – makes it so; we know so. There is nothing in this world, which we cannot make happen. My personal belief is that we all are part of the same universal energy. We all have access to the same creative forces as anyone else to utilize this energy. We live our dream everyday in our lives. We have made up our mind. This is what we will have and we work towards it every day.

3. **Action.**
   All the belief in the world will not actually make it happen. There is a great saying that goes something like this. The universe (God) will meet you

if you go to the universe. However, the great thing about this is the universe takes Universe-sized steps to your human steps.

We must take steps to achieve this on our own. Another way to look at this is: If we wish to have something different than we have today, then it follows that we must be a different person to be able to accept this gift.

In other words, the definition of insanity is doing the same thing over and over and expecting different results!

My question to you is what is your dream? Is your dream big enough to excite you? Are there others who share in your dream? (There is a lot of power in groups!) Are you taking the steps as described? And perhaps the biggest test of all – Do others laugh at your dream because they think it is unreachable?

Don't worry! You are on the right track. We call these people dream stealers. They steal other people's dreams from them because they have not figured out how to get their own!

Go Dream!

## **Final Words For Doing**

I do not believe in failure.

---

*T*here is always something good to be found in any learning experience.

---

Besides, if we always succeeded at everything we did, we would not know that we succeeded because there would be nothing to measure success against.

However, no one likes to fail at anything. In order to give your Self the best opportunity to continue moving forward on the *BeDoHave* path, here are four steps to follow:

1. **Define your Self.**
   Who are you? What do you stand for? What are the values that make you whole? Begin this task immediately and put it in writing. Refer to it often. Refine it continually as you discover unknown things about your Self. Start with the following premise, which many of us have. You are not your work, your family or anything else external. You are internal. You are you.

2. **Define your dream for the future:**
   This is your intent. If it remains undefined and unrecognized, it will most likely never be created into reality. The reason for this is that you have to create your own reality. If you do not begin with

this first step of intent to create, nothing will be able to happen. Everything that has ever been created was first a thought; then it was spoken, and then acted upon. Of course this concept is much easier said than done. May I suggest you not concern your Self with the how it is to be done and only concern your Self with the intent? After you are clear with the intent, and begin to take action, the Universe will step in with much of the how. It is magic!

3. **Live as if each minute were your last.**
This has been said so many times that we normally brush the thought aside. Why do we do this? It is a crucial part of happiness and joy. We have a tremendous power within us to change our world. I believe strongly we create our own world by making each choice that is offered to us every second of the day. That is the ONLY power we have; but it is an incredible power! When we decide to consciously choose to make each and every decision, then we are creating our world on a minute-by-minute basis. Making our choices becomes easier! Simply follow the guidelines as you defined who you are in step 1!

4. **Let it go.**
We have no power over the future! You can worry, fret, get ulcers, scream, shout, and go down kicking; but you will not be able to alter your future one bit. More importantly, while you are making that fuss about the future, you might miss making a couple of crucial, conscious

choices in the here and now which will allow you to create your future!

# ⋘ Have ⋙

We are so obsessed with doing that we have no time and no imagination left for being. As a result, men are valued not for what they are but for what they do or what they have-for their usefulness.

Thomas Merton

## **Introduction To Have**

I have all that I need. In fact, there is abundance in my life. There is more of almost everything in my life these days - money, joy, people, and ideas. I notice increases in other ways as well, which include sorrow, things to do, clients, and partners.

To what can I point a finger and say - this is the reason?

*Do you have a desire for more in your life?*

I believe there is a simple explanation for this abundant phase. In some way, I asked for it to be my reality.

1. There is plenty in the world as it is. In fact, there always will be plenty.
2. The universe is made of energy and you can create what you want from this energy.
3. Everything that is - started with a thought.
4. You can think!

Abundance is right in front of you.

Ask and ye shall receive.

Of course, it is not simple, but it is the answer.

---

*H*aving what you need, even having abundance, is the inevitable result of being true to who you are, and doing what you love to do.

---

As we work towards these two goals, the tools we use allow us to have all we need. In the beginning, our basic needs are met. Afterwards, we create abundance from a place of gratitude for what we have, and from the knowledge that we can create whatever we want.

This all begins with the steps, which we have discussed to this point.

There is a path each of us must follow in order to reach the point where we can create abundance.

Ego equals personality.

I believe each of us has an ego and a soul, and the two must be balanced for us to be happy as people.

The reasons are clear: We are born with a calling. Our souls have a mission in life. In fact, many teachers say it is the whole reason we are here.

However, to enable us to perform our mission, or our *calling* in life, we have a body. To control our body and to be a "person," each of us develops an ego, or personality. Our personality has its own requirements.

These requirements are quite familiar to us. Each of us has basic needs to be met if we are to function as human beings. These needs can be classified into eight groups, and tied to a "path of development" each of us must progress as we live our life. In other words, the ego/personality has to grow and evolve along a known path. Additionally, you can place your Self on the path to understand where you might be.

Here they are:

**Stop the pain.**
At the very lowest level, there is some sort of pain. It could be emotional, physical, or psychologycal. When this pain is bad enough, nothing else matters.

**Safety, food, shelter.**
These are the needs we all have, and must fulfill before advancing to the next step. Some people will spend their entire lives working a job that they do not care for, in a place they dislike, and associate with others of like mind because they are able to meet these basic needs. They do not realize there are other choices.

**Belonging, love, needs.**
With this group, we begin to move into the area of the soul. We all desire to belong. We all want to be loved and to love. If each of us were able to clearly understand our individual needs, and work to get them met, what a world it would be!

**Integrity, standards, Self-esteem.**

Are you seeing the pattern? As we are complete in one area, we are given the ability to see into the next. Someone struggling to put food on the table and a roof over their heads is unable to be concerned about Self-esteem or integrity!

**Community, network.**

Now, we begin to reach out to others as we fulfill our basic needs. Our ego is being satisfied, (if it has not run wild,) and we are able to help others.

**Integrate career, life.**

At this point, we are able to begin to listen to our soul. What is it saying to us? What are we being asked to do? It is common in the United States for people who have reached a certain age and success level to wake up one day and realize they are doing the wrong job! Some try to ignore this call of the soul. The soul can become very insistent, and do drastic things to get attention! Disease is many times a result of not following your soul's calling.

**Peace, happiness, and effortless life.**

Is this where we all wish to be? We all have the ability. We all have the skills. I think we must realize some people reach this level as homeless wanderers, while some reach this place as mothers and/or housewives. The key is to know you are there. It is not about money, power, and things.

**Contribution, teach/mentor/Self-actualization.**

We all have read and studied many of people who have become teachers. You probably know a couple. These people have reached the stage of development where they understand exactly who they are, and where they are going, and are completely at ease with that knowledge. They create their own life, instead of waiting to see what life brings to them. They are our teachers, our mentors, and the people you turn to for help and direction in your own development.

Are you able to place your Self somewhere on this path? Are you able to see the different steps of this path in others? Do you see where you want to be?

You have the power to get there.

# Five Steps To A Great Life!

Here are five crucial steps to 'having' the life you want.

1. **Have Gratitude.**
   Gratitude opens the door for all which follows. Have gratitude for where you are and how you got there. Give thanks for what you have and those around you.

2. **Acceptance**
   Can you accept that you are where you are because of the choices you have made? Every choice combined together has created the life you now have. You may not have been aware of the choice you were making, but it was a choice just the same. No choice is a choice too!

   Accept the idea your life is perfect as it is. Not to say it is wonderful, or perfection, but it is perfect in the sense that you created it, and therefore, you can change it if you want.

3. **Choice**
   Begin to make conscious choices on a consistent basis. Hold every decision to your values and definitions of success as a measuring tool. This will begin to create a life based on what calls to you and what you have defined as success to you.

4. **Let go of the outcome**
   The challenging part of all this is giving up the idea that you have any other control of your future! If you define success as money, or a job, or a

relationship, then you are likely to be disappointed. Life never gives us what we want, but what we deserve.

As soon as we decide to create a life based on what is most important to us, then we must let go of the outcome and trust that those decisions will bring to us what we need.

If each of us creates a world that fulfills us based on our values, and we feel successful based on internal (and controllable) instead of external (and uncontrollable) rewards, then we can be successful without money, or relationships or any other external gratification.

5. **Attract**
What follows is the power of attraction. As you find your life increasingly filled with joy, and happiness, you begin to attract things to you that you need. This may be money or relationships or power.

Here is the difference. Money, relationships and power are not success in themselves, but now you can use these tools to enrich your life as well as others.

## **How Do I Keep Moving?**

The most common challenge I hear is "How do I keep moving in the right direction?"

We all face this question every day. How do we stay on track, keep our focus, and take the baby steps necessary to maintain momentum? It is so easy in our busy lives to allow minor distractions, a crisis, or other people to pull us away from the things that we know we have to do in order to move forward. This can be applied to work, home or Self.

1. **The mindset must be there.**
   We must control the Gremlin that says tomorrow is OK. The decision to accomplish our goals has to be firmly made in advance and not every day or you will spend all your time convincing your Self to get moving!

2. **There must be a plan of action.**
   This is the goals step. How can you steer your life if you don't have a clear idea of where you are going? How can you make minor corrections in your path if you don't have a benchmark to measure against! Goals must be clear, set against a timeframe and then broken down into manageable daily or weekly benchmarks that you reach. If you can't reach these daily tasks, then revisit your plan. There is something out of whack. Either you really don't desire your goals enough, they are too high, or too much for you at this time. Adjust your goals in order for them to become reachable. It is very important to meet your benchmarks. That feeling of satisfaction is

crucial to your well-being and getting up and doing it again tomorrow!

3. **Desire!**
Do you really want what achieving your goals will bring you! How badly? Write it down. Be very explicit. Our minds will work subconsciously to assure us of success in our endeavors if we have shown it the reason and the way!

4. **Accountability.**
Somehow, we have to make ourselves accountable. There are lots of ways to accomplish this. A journal is a great start. Tell your Self what you will do in your writings. Enlist a friend, a spouse or anyone who can say to you -tell me- did you accomplish your goals today?

I have allowed my life to be busy to the point that my goals are getting crowded out, with missed benchmarks. This affects my mental state as I do not get the freedom of knowing I am on the right path. This lack of completeness in turn affects everything I do. Therefore, I must read my own words and take action.

How about you?

## **What If?**

Let us play a game, albeit a very serious one, of *what if.*

*What if* is an extremely important tool to be used as you go through life.

You should always be asking your Self – what if?

For instance:

What if I decided today was the day I was to tackle the one big challenge, which I have been facing: (exercise, finances, relationship, job satisfaction, happiness, stress). If I were to stay at it until it was resolved – what would my life be like?

What if I decided to follow my instincts, and determined to change the career path I was on? Do I see a future there worth the effort it would take?

What if I stay where I am, where will I be in ten years? Does that appeal to me?

What if I changed my attitude, how would that affect my life? Does my present attitude bring me the kind of life I desire?

What if I lost my means of income today? How would I be financially, and do I have a backup plan?

What if I lost my loved one or ones today? Would I believe we had parted saying all I needed to say?

What if I shared all my feelings with my life partner? Would that make our relationship stronger – or not?

These things do happen. Fortunately, we are given incredible means with which to deal with all of them. We even have the capabilities to look at the future and to prepare for the future. The key is to make use of those gifts!

There is no sadder thing than to hear someone say – If only I had...

## **Don't Look Back**
## (Except to Measure!)

At times, we get overwhelmed. No matter how hard you work at your to-do list, there is always more to add to the bottom of the list. And, since life is ever-changing, something new requiring attention is always on the horizon - or in your face. There is nothing wrong with this; it's just the way it goes.

The challenge is in realizing a sense of completion, taking pride in finishing a job, or a project even if there is another one waiting to be done.

Here is my suggestion. Stop and look back. Take the time to remember all you have done. Celebrate the completions of projects and goals. Enjoy the crossing out of the items on the to-do list. We tend to run down the road so fast that we forget to remember where we have been, what we have seen, and what we have done.

Looking back and taking count is an excellent stress reliever as well. If you are the type of person that allows your Self to build up a stress level looking at all the things you have yet to do, I would bet you are not taking the time to look back at all the things you have done! Sure there is more to do. There will always be more to do.

Be careful though because it is so easy to get caught up in the past. We all know people who live there. For some reason, they do not wish to live in the present time. These people are easy to spot. Any conversation with them will quickly turn to how much better things used to be. The problem with this thinking is the unreality of it!

---

*The past is just that -the past - and as such, it is gone and never to return.*

---

We were given the ability to create our lives by our thoughts. We are also given the ability to do this every single second of our lives! Every second is a brand new opportunity to create something the way we want it. How much better could it be?

I encourage you to use your to-do lists, and your project lists, and your daily activities to actively create what you truly want for your Self. Then look back every now and then to measure where you are, how you are doing, and to celebrate how far you have come.

## **Make Room**

Have you asked for something more or something different to happen for you in your life? Did you know that you need to make room for the new things that are coming?

How do you make this room? Brutally, Specifically, Without fear, Carefully, and Completely.

Look at your life very carefully. Look for things, emotions and people who are no longer adding to your existence and remove them.

Search for:

<u>Clothing</u> you haven't worn in a year. Give it away.

<u>Goals</u> you will not achieve. Delete them from your list.

<u>Items</u> on your to do list that are not getting done. Either do them or delete them.

<u>People</u> who are dragging you down or holding you back. Say goodbye.

<u>Emotions</u> that are a weight you are carrying around:

<u>Guilty feelings</u> – Why are you guilty? Do whatever you have to do to get rid of it. Confess if you have done something and ask forgiveness. Then forget it. If you hurt someone, apologize and get over it!

<u>Anger</u> – Why are you angry? Search it out. Come to terms. If you can do something about then do it. If you cannot, let it go! Anger is one of the worst (and most common) energy drainers around. If you are angry how will you be grateful for what you have?

<u>Jealousy</u> - Of what or whom are you jealous? Go talk to the person you are jealous of and tell them. It will make their day and you will get over it. Then if you want something bad enough, go get it your Self!

These steps are not difficult to do, and the rewards are incredible.

*Be Do Have*

## **Resist Nothing – What A Concept**

Thaddeus Golas' <u>The Lazyman's Guide to Enlightenment</u> is a wonderful book. This work explains his concept of "Resist Nothing." I am very attracted to this concept.

Consider the following passage from Tao Te Ching - a 2500 year-old work written by Lao tse:

"When we learn to work with our own Inner Nature, and with the natural laws operating around us, we reach the level of Wu Wei. Then we work with the natural order of things and operate on the principle of minimal effort. Since the natural world follows that principle, it does not make mistakes. Mistakes are made - or imagined - by man, the creature with the overloaded Brain who separates himSelf/herSelf from the supporting network of natural laws by interfering and trying too hard."

I thought this to be another wonderful illustration of Golas' concept of "resists nothing." If the natural world follows the principle of minimal effort, which to me sounds a lot like no resistance, then it makes sense that by interfering and trying too hard, we can actually get in our own way.

As an example of this, Shelly and I signed a contract to buy that small horse farm that I mentioned earlier in my book. As I look back on the eight-week process, I realize that it could have been a very trying experience, with forces not in our control holding up other decisions and plans, and the tension and fears that normally accompany this type of major purchase and change in lifestyle.

We realized that by accepting the process, having no resistance, and allowing things to work out on their own, we were at peace for the greater part of the time. We consciously chose to allow whatever happened to happen and looked for the best. Every decision made by us was based on values and definitions of our success. Therefore, we are living our lives based on our definitions of values and success, and not allowing the process of buying a property to control us. We left the outcome in the hands of some other Power that has that control. We resisted nothing.

It was a wonderfully freeing experience and not one we could have done ten years ago.

The point is this:

The next time you feel resistance, stop! Take a moment and ask your Self why you are resisting. Is it fear of the unknown, or fear of loss? Could it be there is something there you need to learn? Is there something that you do not want to go through that might be a perceived pain or change? Is it an argument that you must win to be right? Maybe your energy comes from tension?

---

*Think oak tree and bend in the wind.*

---

"We are equal beings and the universe is our relations with each other. The universe is made of one kind of entity:

Each one is alive. Each determines the course of his own existence."

Thaddeus Golas

## **Create A Life Equation**

Each of us desires health, happiness, and financial security. We know there are ingredients that produce these qualities for us.

Let's look at some common ones, with examples, and see how these might work for you. An interesting challenge is to create word equations to help make these ideas crystal clear to you.

Consistent savings + time = Retirement Fund

We all know the phrase "Pay your Self first." It is suggested that you decide on a percentage you are going to save every month and pay it to the savings account before you pay your bills. After all, who is more important here? One day you will look back and be amazed at how it adds up. Compound interest is what makes this financial idea so attractive.

Revenue + low expenses = Profit

Last year, at this time, we had just moved. The reason that my wife and I moved was to lower our expenses. After the mortgage, utilities, maintenance and traveling costs were totaled; we added over $600 every month to our budget.

Set aside a couple of hours to look closely at your expenses for last year. (You do have your expenses for last year, don't you?) Play a game and say – If I had to cut expenses by 50% what would I do? Then cut your expenses by 25%.

*Be Do Have*

Look at your sources of income. How can you supplement or increase them? Ask for more income from your job? Be better at what you do? Change careers? Turn a hobby into a part-time income?

Added value + service = Referrals

From experience, I can tell you that this absolutely works. I strive to give more than expected and add value to my services – no matter what that service is! In the first place, who wants to do mediocre work?

Secondly, there is a huge benefit to your Self-esteem knowing that you have done your best without expectation of return in kind. Think what the world would be like if everyone did. My business is built on referrals from people I have associated with or affected in some way.

Self-respect + Self-care = Self-Esteem

---

*A*ll growth begins with basic personal foundation principles such as values, boundaries, reserves, and tolerations.

---

We must take care of ourselves emotionally, physically, and energetically in order to have a strong base with which we need to grow and prosper. Self-respect comes from doing those things for ourselves that make us know who we are – and it shows us that it is good to be proud of it!

Plan + consistent action = Results

Make your plan and work your plan. We have heard this said repeatedly. There is a reason the phrase is repeated so often.

Consistent action + results = Momentum

Once we start down the road of action, and begin to see the results, brand new opportunities arise; people and "coincidences" begin appearing, which we never before could see. Some people call this luck. Bah! Humbug! We make our luck.

How do you like these formulas? I have found them simple but effective. Make up your own. You are not limited to two words, either. Here is another example, which is one of my formulas:

Skills + marketing − fear = Business success

I have skills and marketing abilities but fear sometimes stands in my way.

Use these formulas or make up your own as a reminder of what needs attention for you.

## A huge part of the 'having' is 'giving'

Somewhere along my path I finally completely understood the reasons behind giving (as if there has to be a reason.) It's not the only reason, but for me, it was very powerful and eye opening.

*Be Do Have*

The lesson came from Neale Donald Walsh, in his book <u>Communion with God</u>. I highly recommend the book, even if you may not agree with all he says.

Mr. Walsh wrote: "Since we are all one, when you give to someone you are, in essence, giving to your Self." Interesting, I thought! I had certainly never thought giving to others was a gift to me.

He also wrote about the harm a person does when they give too much, as in a co-dependency situation that does not allow a person to evolve into himSelf or herSelf; to be who they need to be. Pain might be part of their growth and if you take away too much of that pain, you are getting in the way of a natural learning process. Since we are all one, if you give too much to one person, you are getting in the way of your own growth!

For instance, give food to a hungry person, but teach them how to feed themselves. (Haven't I heard that somewhere?) This is something that I have kept in mind as I do what I can to be of help. I volunteer in a manner that makes best use of my talents. I have realized the benefits to me are far beyond the effort I give. My rewards include gratitude from my clients and peers, building my own confidence in my abilities, a much larger network of people, and lots more opportunities.

## **Give A Little, Get A Lot**

As you begin to put all these systems in place in your life, you will realize your needs and wants are being fulfilled. Sometimes your fulfillment can be more than you bargained for in the first place. Sometimes you get overwhelmed!

Not too long ago, I had to stop what I was doing. All of it!

I realized my mind was beginning to shut down on me, little by little. I found my Self angry with no apparent reason at little things or even nothing. I was forgetful, edgy, and seemed unable to communicate properly, or to be able to finish a project.

So – I shut down. I sort of turned everything off and rebooted. Afterwards, I stopped and looked around at where I was and what I was doing and re-evaluated my projects and workload. I looked for things I was tolerating and began to eliminate them. I worked a bit on my core set of values, redefining them and ensuring that the things I was doing were in line with my own set of values and not someone else's. I looked at my needs, defining these once more, and striving to get those met.

Most of this took place more or less internally, although as I look back I can see clearly now just what was happening.

With a new dedication, and after a breather, there is a new bounce in my step and clarity to my thoughts. We all need to do this from time to time.

---

*K eep focused on not only where you are going, but where you are.*

---

The present is where we live. It is great to invest your Self fully into today for a dream tomorrow, but don't forget when tomorrow comes, if you don't take some time in order to appreciate it there will never be a today! You will always be living for tomorrow!

Keep tabs on your inner feelings as they talk to you constantly, keeping you aware of how to take care of you. Remember – no one else can do this but you! Your subconscious talks to no one but you!

As we travel this path called life, each of us wants to be successful at something. We have already learned how to define success for us. Here in the 'Have' portion of the book, we need to revisit success one more time.

## Are You Successful?

I have spent many hours and tons of energy striving to be successful. I have used success as a reason for being away from my family, explaining away my grumpy moods and being hard on those with whom I work.

I allowed my lack of success to increase stress and times of feeling down. My children have felt the pressures of this stress as many things I taught them were clouded by my desire for them to be successful later on in their life.

I targeted success with money. If I only had money, and lots of it, I would then be successful! Finally, I realized this is exactly what most of us do.

Now, I know this idea of success being equal to money is completely false. I have always been successful and exactly what I should have been. You see, there are no *should have, could have,* scenarios. We are what we are at any point in our lives. If at that point, we find that we want to be someone or something else – then we can change.

Before you make any changes, consider the cost of the change. After weighing the total cost of the change versus the benefits gained, you can decide the change is worth the effort and expense. After you get accustomed to thinking in this way, the decision will be an easy one. If you decide the cost is more than you are willing to pay, then maybe you are already on the right path and need to readjust your thinking in order to accept and be grateful for where you already are.

Be careful as you look at your life. We tend to compare our lives to somebody else's life (like on TV.) We are comparing with someone that appears to be better, but in fact would like to be just like us. You do not know what lives people truly live.

In our family, we have discussed this phenomenon at great length. We decided that we would continue to ask for more abundance in our life. At the same time, we are actively reducing the amount of money we spend without affecting the quality of our lives to allow us more freedom of time. We want more time together!

We have decided that we are successful in every definition of the word. My wife and I have more than enough money, a nice roof over our heads, comfortable, reliable transportation, a great circle of support and friendship, a wonderful marriage and children; oh yes, and plenty to eat.

Again, it seems everything comes back to choice. The choices we make are the ones that create our life. If we choose to be successful...If we choose to live by our values...If we choose to be happy.

Why do we make the choices we do? I think it goes deep within us.

The relationship between our soul and our ego has everything to do with how we live our life. It has been talked about at least as far back as Plato, in The Republic, who said "a person's soul chooses its parents, and their life, and the conditions it will be born into, in order to manifest the destiny the soul desires."

I have come to believe very strongly through research, study and personal experience that each of us has a purpose or a destiny to fulfill.

Unfortunately, once we are born, we forget that purpose. We must first learn our way around in the environment we have chosen. For instance, your purpose may be to teach others they have a choice. First, however, you must learn this your Self. This lesson might come easily and it might come hard after 40 or more years! But after you learn your purpose in life, the reason your soul is here, you will have found your calling. As soon as you follow that path, that calling, and you will be working in harmony with your soul's desires. Life will become filled with purpose and you will have much less of a struggle. I believe this is why most of us do not seriously question our lives until we reach our 30s and 40s. Is this where mid-life crisis come from?

---

*With the exception of some genius-like people, who find their soul purpose very early in life, most of us must follow the path that our ego wants before we can find the path that our soul desires.*

---

We spend out time with our parents developing this ego, and the first years on our own seeking gratification for the ego. This gratification comes from money, power, titles, cars, houses and other materialistic things that are so important to the ego. This is good, for we must have balance in our lives between the ego and the soul.

The soul realizes this and waits patiently for the ego to fulfill its desires. But, the soul is always there in the background, with a very small voice letting you know what it wants. The problem is – and you have heard this many times - is that we never listen well enough to hear it!

As we mature, the soul will want to be heard. This could come in various ways and strengths, from feelings of unease about your work or personal relationships, to absolute knockdown blows like cancer or an accident. The soul will let you know that it is time to pay attention!

We need to know and understand the desires of both the soul and the ego, and work to balance the two together. Most of us would be unable to completely dedicate ourselves to the soul's work, and leave the ego (and the body that houses it) to fend alone.

We all need the basics of life.

Here is some good news. After you have met your basic ego needs, you have learned your soul's desires, and have made a conscious effort to fulfill those desires; the universe will step forward to help you with the ego needs.

In other words, if you take care of your soul, your soul (which is part of the universal energy) will take care of you.

---

*O r, be who you are, do what you love and you will have what you need.*

---

When I say you will have what you need, I do not mean you can sit in front of the TV eating potato chips and waiting for what you want to arrive by mail. We still must define, plan and apply ourselves. Through this process comes growth and progress along our paths.

# **About Goals**

There are two basic ways to pursue your goals. One is to attack, the other attract. Let's take a quick look at both.

Attack!

The attack method is by far the most commonly used and taught today. In attack mode, goals are clearly defined in one, three, five and even ten-year increments. The reasons behind the goals (the why) are specifically stated in order to help ensure that there is enough drive to complete the task at hand. Steps are then crafted on a daily basis with checkpoints along the way. These steps will enable measurement of progress and corrective action, which will keep you on the path, thereby bringing about completion of the goals.

This method works. Many of us need the support, structure, commitment and organization that a goal-oriented process produces. However, there is another way.

Attract!

This method is next in the evolution of achieving what you want from life. The difference is instead of working specifically toward a goal or a set of goals in order to realize success in a predetermined timeframe; you can let all of that go. Instead, you can base your work on less defined criteria.

For instance, what if you lived your life doing only what was fun? Or, what if you did only that which brought joy? Perhaps your choice would be attracting business instead of working as hard as you are now to get business.

In order to accomplish this as a salesperson, you might stop all your networking activities. You might even stop all cold-calling. Instead, you could try to focus on providing extraordinary service, helping existing clients in any way possible, or going out of your way to build relationships for the joy of it instead of for the business. Instead of selling clients, you might decide to concentrate on educating them and helping them be the best they can be at their work.

In this way, you begin to attract business to you instead of going out to get it. The attraction method is a natural progression from the goal-oriented process and it can actually be used simultaneously. As you evolve, learn and grow, you will find your Self naturally using attraction more and more in your life.

If you are interested in using attraction in your life, here are some other suggestions to measure by:

- Has to be something I have never done before
- Has to afford me freedom
- Has to pay extraordinarily well
- Has to make a huge impact
- Has to be an adventure

## **More About Goals**

So you have set your goals for the year. Congratulations!

Unfortunately, most of us set our goals for incorrect reasons. We set goals for short-term objectives. Most of these objectives concern materialistic wants: money, and physical things.

Now, let's look at a slightly different approach.

---

Start with deciding what your life should be. Take some time to define your life five years from now. Define your life and the way you'd like it to be in five years.

1. What am I feeling?
   _____
   _____

2. What types of people are around me?
   _____
   _____

3. What are my surroundings like?
   _____
   _____

> 4. What am I doing?
>    _____
>    _____
>
> 5. Where am I going?
>    _____
>    _____
>
> 6. Where have I been?
>    _____
>    _____

Notice that there are no questions dealing with money, named places, or named people. The answers to these questions will provide you with attitudes, feelings, values, perceptions and other non-tangible ideas that make life worth living no matter where you are, who you are with, or what you are doing!

If we have created a lifestyle that we like, then the physical part of our lives will fit right in and accompany the lifestyle because it has to! Look at the lifestyle you want to create, and set your plan to achieve the lifestyle instead if the physical side of life most of us set our goals to achieve.

To go even deeper, define your values very clearly. Make certain that your vision of your life in five years fits with your values. Is it worth it? You have heard the phrase, "plan your work and work your plan?"

If you do not create your life by setting goals and a plan to reach them, someone will be doing the setting and planning for you. If you think about it, that is really scary!

What type of vision do they have for you?

Think of it this way. Look back five years ago in your life.

---

*A*re you today where you imagined you would be five years ago? Or are you where someone else imagined you would be?

---

Don't you think your life would dramatically improve if you made the plan? Don't you think you might have a little more interest in your life than someone else? I should hope you would.

As the advertisement says so well: Just Do it!

In 1996, I asked my Self these questions and wanted answers:

"Why am I here?"
"What am I supposed to be doing?"
"Why do I have this feeling of being lost?"

My family and I have recently completed sailing for seven years. We traveled many miles up and down the East Coast and the Caribbean Islands in a thirty-six foot sailboat. In fact, we lived a life many people dream of living. Our first son was born in Tortola, British Virgin Islands. We ate fresh fish caught from the back of the boat. Our clothes were shorts, T-shirts and flip-flops. We worked when we needed money, and traveled when we did not. My wife and I met wonderful people, living the same life as we were.

However, something was missing: money, or rather the things money could bring us. Our egos wanted us to taste the comforts that money could provide. We wanted material things, such as rental cars and trips back to the States for visiting - even a bigger sailboat.

We (the family) sold our boat and returned to the United States in order to do some things that would feed our egos! During those five years, some amazing things have happened.

First and most important is that we now understand the difference and significance of ego and soul. My wife, Shelly and I understand that the journey is the most important part, and not the getting there. (That is because you never get there!) And now we clearly understand that our reality is controlled by only us. That control is managed by the choices we make.

After all this became clear, it was easy to see that my soul's work is to share that knowledge with everyone possible. This revelation led me to coaching, and writing. Interestingly enough, since I am doing what I am supposed to be doing, I am extremely comfortable with who I am and what I do. Every day is a pleasure. There is something good in everything that comes to me. Finances are not a problem. Relationships are not a challenge. (Well, maybe except with my eleven-year-old. Where does he get that music?)

I have learned to trust my intuition much more and to place faith in the power of the Universe, which will assist me in all I do. The attention focused on improving all aspects of my own personal foundation - including knowing personal values, eliminating tolerations, understanding and meeting my needs and living for today instead of tomorrow or yesterday - has made such a difference in my quality of life that it is almost unbelievable.

Is our life perfect now? Life will never be perfect. The truth is that there are too many outside influences. There is always the balancing act between the soul and the ego. Give and take of being able to do and have it all will always exist. However, the quality of my life is vastly improved even from the idyllic days of cruising in our sailboat over beautiful clear Bahamian waters with perfect weather, owing no one, with no one to answer to on a daily basis. (We might go back, by the way.)

I want for you to be able to see that these methods of living work – I would like you to realize this for your Self. You were put here for a purpose. If you can find that purpose, and follow that calling, no matter what it is, you will be richly rewarded. At that time, heaven on earth will become your reality.

I want for you - Heaven on Earth.

Our story is the story we are telling. Shelly and I have heaven on earth. This heaven is an ongoing creation made by our daily choices. The rest of this book is examples of the things, which I believe are crucial to having what you want.

Please realize this is from my perspective, and may not be true for you. Then again, it just might be true.

## Reality #1:  Dreams carry a price that must be paid.

My wife and I decided that we wanted horses. You know, a horse farm, in the country, with rolling fields of deep green grass, a handsome barn, full of sweet smelling hay and shavings for the stalls. The barn would have a separate room for the well-oiled and well-worn saddles. Inside the barn would be tack so that we could throw the saddle on one of the horses and go for a ride whenever we desired.

Of course, we would also probably need a round pen where we could exercise and train the horses…and maybe a riding arena when needed. Our vision was of a farm with a clear and deep lake. We wanted the lake on the farm to be full of fish, with an overflow in order to keep the bubbling creek running.

Shelly and I received all of the things that we wanted to be included in this vision! Only it isn't quite like the dream. For starters, the field is a bit overgrown with pine scrub and weeds that have grown into trees with thorns! I don't remember ever seeing briars an inch thick before!

Somehow the rain runoff has managed to create these red clay gullies in the field. The gullies have to be filled in before the horses are delivered so that they don't break their legs. Oh, and the barn that we dreamed of – well, we still have to build it!

The lake is already there! The only downside is the beavers that seem to love all trees except the briars and thorn trees. They do a great job of building dams with our nice trees, which they cut down during the night while we sleep.

The beavers were cute when we got here, but it gets a little old tearing out dams and having them built back that night using our good trees!

Our lake is full of fish though! At least, that is what I heard. My problem is that I have been too busy to go fishing.

We are beginning to understand the snickers and laughs we get when people find out what we are doing with the farm. How much work can it be to design, lay out and build a 36 foot by 84 foot barn that contains 10 stalls, an office, a tack room, hay storage, a wash rack and a feed room? You mean we have to wash these horses too?

On the other hand, the benefits are all there for us. We are getting in shape! Shelly and I are not frivolously wasting our money on something silly like a vacation. The boys are learning the joys of working as a family. We are all experiencing the wonders of spending time in the great outdoors.

All kidding aside, the lesson comes home again as it did when we were building the sailboat that we would sail and live on for over seven years – dreams have a price. In my opinion, there is no question the price is well worth it.

After dinner, not too long ago, my family and I sat out on the two-story deck. We looked out over the field that we had spent the day clearing. The brush bonfire was still burning down, and the stars and the moon rose in the clear night in all their glory. As we sat on our deck as a family and talked about what was to come, there was a clear consensus from all – we wouldn't have it any other way.

*Be Do Have*

## **Reality #2: You must keep going no matter what.**

A while back, when you looked from our back porch, down across the round pen that we built right after we moved in, all that was to be seen was woods and brush. It was thick in there, with lots of brambles, and briars and it was sort of swampy where the beavers had dammed up the creek in several places and flooded the woods.

One of the projects we knew had to be done was to clear that land. Afterwards, we felt that we needed to drain the land and plant grass on it for the horses. Our project had to be finished before winter to allow time for growth through the wet winter season. This was a big project to say the least. With any luck at all, the horses will have some grass next spring and summer.

It wasn't easy. It never is when you have a goal that truly means something to you. A price had to be paid both financially and personally. We burnt stumps, debris and logs steady for three weeks. My family and I were heartily sick of fires and smoke. We spent many hours picking up sticks and roots out of the fields and carrying them to the fires. Literally tons of ashes and moved tons of mud were buried. We started in the dark before 6:30 in the morning and worked an hour or two and then went back in the evening until after dark. (We had to make a living too!)

However, I can tell you it is a tremendously satisfying experience to complete an undertaking of something of this magnitude. The rewards of working with family are also huge.

But again, it wasn't easy. If I had looked at the whole project, I might not have even begun when I did, or at all. If I had worried about finishing the project, or paying for it, or whether we could finish it before the winter rains, I might never have begun either. If I had listened to well meaning friends, I might never have believed it possible. If we had gone off and done all the fun things that we were invited to do, or left the projects to do another day, we would never have realized our dreams.

There is only one way that I know to do this big a project. Are you ready for the secret?

Just do it.

Have faith that you can. Start immediately. Work at it every moment you can. Work only on what is in front of you – do the things that need to be done now. You will know what that will be. Do not concern your Self with tomorrow, or next week, or what the end will be like. Just do it. And keep doing it until you are done.

Then, you too will enjoy the wonderful feeling of accomplishment and satisfaction that comes with having done something that most could or would not have done. It takes no special talent, nor trade, nor money, nor strength, nor experience, nor brains to realize these truths. It takes will to gain from these methods that I teach – it takes choice. Every single person has those two tools.

---

*T he size of the project or goal really does not matter. The steps are the same. Just do it.*

---

*Be Do Have*

## Reality #3: Watch for natural laws…When you pour it rains.

One of the next steps was *concrete pouring day* for the barn footings. After footings go in, there is a strong permanent foundation needed for the structure. It gives one a feeling of having finally gotten underway with the actual building. Of course, there is a great deal of work to be done prior to this event but actually pouring concrete is like burning the proverbial bridge. As soon as that stuff hardens, there is no turning back. In a way, it is a commitment to finish the project.

In the days prior to the concrete being poured, it rained. A lot. It was the first rain that we had in eight weeks! The footings were full of water and red clay mud. Our dirt road that led to the barn was slippery, slushy, and full of red clay. We thought we'd have to cancel the concrete truck and get out the shovels, move the schedule for everything else back at least three days while hoping that the sun would come out and dry the mud enough to drive on it.

Does this happen to you? Of course it does. That is life itSelf. Instead of brooding about life, we need to move steadily forward, working hard on our plans, dreams and goals. Excitement builds, confidence improves, and fears melt away as progress is apparent. We tell others how well we are doing, how easy it is, and paint rosy pictures of the future. Then BAM! Out of nowhere, the Universe steps in and says…wait just a minute. Take three steps back. Go directly to jail. Lose a turn. Confidence tumbles. Can I really do this? It is too hard? Why bother? Excitement evaporates. I can't believe I have to do THAT all over again. And, of course, all the people to whom you bragged about the future will surely turn up right now and ask how things are going. They might even ask you if it is worth it.

It is worth it?

Remember this: Nothing worth having is free (except love!) Natural law is this: Everything worth having must be paid for; not always with money, but somehow, we all pay a price for the things that we truly want. Do you desire a wonderful life or a long successful relationship with a perfect mate? You must work at it. Would you like to have financial freedom, or time freedom? There is a price to be paid.

Most are not willing to pay the price. They say it is too high. It is a personal choice, but when you get to the finish and look back, the efforts made look less difficult than they did when you first began your project.

When you are ready to do something or to accomplish something, just start by doing one thing, which will bring it to fruition. You might not know where to begin, but do anything to get underway.

Next, look for that moment when you are "pouring the concrete," so to speak. Look for that defining step that says you are committed to toil on and don't stop. By doing so, you make turning back more difficult. Keep at it; step-by-step and day-by-day, you will achieve your goal. Try to make the journey an adventure to be enjoyed instead of seeing only the long road ahead to the final reward.

And remember: When you pour, it rains!

## **Reality #4: Define the Dream.**

Do you have a dream? Is there something you want to do, to achieve, or to complete? How close are you? How many people have you told about it? Do you have a written plan on how to get there? And the most important question – Are you taking action?

This much is absolutely true: If you never vocalize your dreams, if you never come up with even the most rudimentary plan on achieving them; and if you never take action, those dreams will never happen.

Many times in my life, I have come up with a dream that appealed to me and then I did what it took to make it come true for me. The most important part is that no one made it happen but me. Sure, I had quite a bit of help along the way. And yes, there were many apparent lucky breaks just when they seemed to be needed the most. This will happen to you as well.

Let me tell you why. We are part of the energy of the Universe. This energy that makes up the Universe answers to us in a way. In fact, the Universe wants desperately to help us in any way possible. The reason for this is simple. We are that energy.

*When we express a desire, and then take action towards that desire, the Universe has no choice but to help us achieve it. That assistance will come in ways that we would have never dreamed. But come, it will!*

One of our latest goals was to complete a roof on our new barn. To you, this goal might not sound like a lot, but I assure you it is. To complete this goal, we had to clear more than two acres of land. After the land was cleared, we had to clean it up and plant grass. 4500 feet of siding lumber had to be cut from the logs and stacked to air dry. Over 60 stumps, and the roots and debris from the trees had to be piled and burned. The barn had to be designed, drawn and all the materials bought and delivered. (By the way, this is not a small barn. It has 10 stalls with two 1100 square foot apartments over it!)

We began this process in the spring of 2003.

When winter brought the cold wet weather, I was very grateful to have completed this part, and we are eager to get on to the next dream of a finished barn, full of horses and trainers.

For every dream turned reality for us over the last 35 years, I can point to several things that are common:
1. Don't be afraid to dream big.
2. Don't listen to others who are afraid.

3. Do make your dream real to you by talking about it and writing it down.
4. Do take action - every day, if possible. Be willing to pay the price!
5. Do not worry about the finish line.
6. Pay attention to what has to be done today.
7. Get that the Universe is working for you, even while you sleep.
8. Don't be afraid to change your goals if you see the need.

Then you too can realize your dreams.

These last two stories are all about choices and how they affect a life. My vision is for every person on the planet to understand how much power they have by making each and every choice consciously to create their lives.

## Choices Make Your Life
### (Whether You Know it or Not!)

It was brought home to me not long ago how important choice is by someone close to me. She is in her early seventies, and recently widowed after 35 + years of marriage. Her life partner had moved on after a two-year battle with cancer.

After a six-month period of grieving where most daily choices were made unconsciously, I began to gently remind her that she had a choice. She could choose to live, or she could choose to join him. She could choose consciously or unconsciously, but either way, a choice would definitely be made.

After eight months, she called to say that she had been to the doctors who had told her about artery blockages in her neck and legs. The doctors told her they would operate. They also told her to begin walking, as the exercise would increase the blood flow enough to force open the arteries. Again, I told her when she did not walk – this was also a choice.

They operated, and as often happens with operations, there were complications. Since that time, she has been in and out of the hospital.

My friend had a mild stroke, losing her speech, balance and memory. Fortunately, she was found quickly and got medical help and is much better, albeit drugged, and in intensive care.

I have to wonder – had she made a choice?

*Be Do Have*

Think hard about this and look at your life. We make choices every single breath we take. Do we take this breath or not? Well, sure you do, but you take it unconsciously. I am asking you to do your best to make every decision a conscious one.

If you will do this consistently, something magical will happen. Your wants will be awarded to you. This will happen because you are creating your life by making choices.

---

*C*hoose to enjoy your life!

---

We have discussed the subject of ego, personality and our soul. This idea of ego and soul being an integral part of our lives might be simpler to understand with a real life story.

Mary is an attractive woman in her early forties. The man she married almost twenty years ago was her second serious relationship in college. Her first "love" (from high school) did not treat her very kindly, taking advantage of her lack of experience in relationships. Mary was raised by a divorced parent. Her mother filled Mary with anger at all men after she finally ended a marriage in which she was completely miserable.

Mary became an over-achiever, striving to show a male-dominated business that she as a woman could and would outperform each and every one. She wore the pants in her new family, and made all the decisions as they began their life together.

She had unconsciously picked her husband due to his passive, non-threatening, and easy-going manner. His ability to accept her as the dominating partner, and tolerate the emotional swings from depression to anger made him seem like the proverbial perfect husband to her.

At thirty-six, when Mother Nature began to place stirrings of motherhood in Mary, she was baffled at first. Later, she embraced the idea as a solution to the questions and longing that welled up continuously within her. She hoped that a baby would solve all the problems.

As you can guess, the baby solved nothing. The Dad is now the Mom as well. Of course, he loves the role. Mary is more lost than ever. Now, in addition to a longing, which she does not comprehend, that grows stronger by the day, she carries a tremendous guilt for not being "a good mother." She works 70 or more hours a week and brings home the money.

However, she does not want to come home any more. Mary is frightened, lonely, completely and hopelessly lost as to her next move. All her planning, all her careful orchestrating to satisfy what she is slowly coming to understand is her ego has her trapped in a corner with no easy way out for her.

So - do you see how the ego worked this whole scenario out? Do you see any evidence of Mary's soul at all?

*Be Do Have*

This is what I see in this particular situation. Mary has lived the Do-Have-Be scenario that many of us struggle with early in our lives. That is: I will *do* these actions, so I can *have* these things, and then I will *be* this person.

Mary married not for love and a relationship, but because her ego told her this man would be the correct person for her. Mary worked hard so that she could *have* the material things she learned made a person successful. Then she hoped that she could *be* somebody. Unfortunately, when the time to *be* came around, her soul was saying, "Nope, that is not who I am!"

This is how I would coach Mary. We would start by helping Mary just be Mary. Then we would work on doing what she loved to do. (It might be what she does.) From that would come the having. As you are *being* who you feel comfortable being and you are *doing* what your soul wants to do, then whatever you *need* will automatically come to you.

First, we would explore what her *values* are. As defined previously, values are intangible activities, preferences or behaviors that attract you. Examples are integrity, relating with God, being the best, being aware, to inspire. For example, if one of Mary's values was integrity, right away, we would know that by not sharing her feelings completely with her husband she is not living in integrity and her Self (soul) would let her know that. (I wonder if it has anything to do with Mary's hair falling out, or the fact that she recently had a very strange severe illness!) Have you heard the term disease?

Next, we would find her *needs*. Each of us has needs, and these needs must be met. I would think Mary has a need to be nurtured and protected. Instead, she picked a man unable to be that strong person. He was also a passive, non-threatening husband, which she thought she wanted.

When our needs are known, the next step is to *consciously* get them met. For Mary, it might be telling her husband and her friends that she needs to be nurtured. By doing this, she would be asking them to nurture her.

If our needs are not met consciously, then we will unconsciously get them met. Sometimes, this works in ways that are very detrimental to our lives! For instance, Mary might find herSelf attracted to another man who she perceives will nurture and protect her.

As a natural process, the next thing that we would work on would be her communication skills. Mary's inability to communicate with her husband has created a scenario that Mary has interpreted as being unsolvable. This might be so, but communication will be no better in the next relationship if not learned here.

Mary is worrying about everyone but Mary. What is going to happen to the child? The husband? Her friends? Her work?

Mary needs to find her *Self.* Mary's Self is being shouted down by Mary's ego. Mary's ego is so afraid that if her Self is heard, Mary will not listen to the ego any more.

The truth is- the ego is right! As soon we find our Self, we learn the dirty tricks that the ego plays on our mind.

I can tell you that this all worked out in the end. Mary and her husband were divorced. Mary has found a life partner with whom she is building a new life, completely aware of all that passed before. She has found joy in being a Mom, and a partner, and has finally learned to listen to her soul's calling.

Mary is *being whom she is, doing what she loves, and is receiving what she needs.*

*I want that for you.*

Do you hear anything calling to you? Are you listening?

## **The Beginning**

Although the book has come to the final chapter, your path has not. As I reread all I have written – (and I have read it *many* times) - I realize that I have simply scratched the surface. There are so many teachers, and so many places to hear this message.

In my opinion, the whole world is on a path to becoming enlightened. I see people all around me reaching for peace instead of violence, love instead of hate and integrity instead of untruths. People everywhere are realizing the joys of BeDoHave. Being who you are, doing what you love and having all you need.

---

*B eDoHave brings immense rewards, both personally and globally. I want these rewards for you.*

---

## **Acknowledgments**

The ideas in this book are not mine. I have been supremely fortunate to have been guided to so many teachers with a great deal of information. Much of the information was corroborated for me by various teachers. Some of these teachers had new and different ideas or thoughts presented in a different light.

If we have written teachings from over 3500 years ago saying the same things we say now, do we not feel the need to have confidence in the truth of those statements?

This book is my take on these teachings and how they have affected my life. I hope it helps you.

This is a list, incomplete I am sure of the most prominent teachers I have had the good fortune to meet, read, or listen to during my journey. Their information may or may not be in this book. I hope that I have credited everybody with anything that I was supposed to recognize.

Jim Rohn said, "Use my stuff. Give me credit the first time, say you heard it somewhere the second time, and take credit the third."

I do not want the credit. I want the teachings heard.

These are in no particular order:
Jim Rohn, Harvey McKay, Jesus, Buddha, M. Scott Peck, Dr. Wayne Dyer, Gary Zukav, Mohammed, Confucius, Richard Bach, Deepak Chopra, Harold Kushner, Don Miguel Ruiz, Jack Kerouac, Napoleon Hill, Thomas Leonard, Sandra

Seich, Neale Donald Walsch, Shakti Gawain, Og Mandino, and so many more. Thank you so very much for coming into my life!

## **Final Thoughts**

Now that you are finished reading, does it clarify anything for you? Is your thinking stimulated? Did you already know all of the information, which I have shared here? Will you use what you already knew, or will you practice what you have learned in this book?

I am always appreciative of your comments, suggestions and even criticisms; they are my inspiration. If after reading this book, you have any questions or comments, please contact me at miami@bedohaveu.com.

Want more? Sign up for free articles, teleclasses and discussion groups at www.bedohaveu.com.

# About The Author

Is it OK if I don't pretend someone else is writing great things about me?

I am just like you. Aren't we all ducks swimming placidly around in the pond of life, although underneath the water, we are all paddling hard just to stay afloat?

My vision is of a world where every single person understands that they can create their life by making conscious choices based on definitions that are true for them alone.

If we all were able to realize the constant joy, and the ability to be happy and fulfilled by following a few simple guidelines, what a world it would be!

Part of my education comes from being a singer/songwriter and learning that music is the Language of the Universe. Have you heard a creek sing?

Building and living on a sailboat with my beautiful wife and son, for seven years taught me the value of responsibility, friendship, and the joy of following the call of my soul.

Since 1999, when I started Creative MasterMinds, many coaching and consulting clients have allowed me to realize the power of opening the mind to new ideas, sharing with others and the incredible results that the power of personal growth offers.

As a result of the commonality of these lessons, in 2004, together with my partner, we created BeDoHave University to share the cure for the unknown American epidemic.

We have built a horse ranch, and bring in people and groups to share the wisdom of horses, and help increase awareness in the importance of teams, leadership, and self-improvement. These skills are also shared in teleclasses, one-on-one and group coaching, and presentations.

Please visit the website at www.BeDoHaveU.com to learn more. If you are interested in exploring coaching, sign up for one of our complimentary coaching calls. (Everybody needs a coach at some point.)

I appreciate you and your support!

Miami Phillips
CEO/Founder
Creative MasterMinds Coaching and Consulting
and Be Do Have University
www.highcountrystables.com
www.bedohaveu.com
www.creativemasterminds.com